LOVE
and
LIFE'S JOURNEY:

Venture in Prayer

D1321717

LOVE
and
LIFE'S JOURNEY:

Venture in Prayer

by

MARK GIBBARD

Society of St John the Evangelist, Oxford

MOWBRAY
LONDON & OXFORD

Copyright © Mark Gibbard 1987

First published 1987
by A. R. Mowbray & Co. Ltd,
Saint Thomas House, Becket Street,
Oxford, OX1 1SJ

Typeset by HiTech Typesetters Ltd, Oxford
Printed in Great Britain by Cox & Wyman Ltd., Reading

British Library Cataloguing in Publication Data

Gibbard, Mark
  Love and life's journey: venture in prayer.
  —— (Mowbray's popular Christian paperbacks)
  1. Prayer
  I. Title
  248.3′2   BV210.2

ISBN 0-264-67052-3

CONTENTS

ACKNOWLEDGEMENTS

The author and publisher wish to express their thanks to the following for permission to reproduce material of which they are the authors, publishers or copyright holders.

Darton Longman & Todd Ltd, London, for extracts from *Contemplative Prayer* by Thomas Merton.

William Collins, Sons & Company Limited, for extracts from *Part of a Journey* by Philip Tonybee (1981), and from *Mister God, this is Anna* (1974).

SCM Press Ltd, for a short extract from Ann and Barry Ulanov, *Primary Speech*, SCM Press 1985.

PREFACE

'I have lived my life as one might follow the flight of a bird. Whatever comes along and demands to be done, when I wake up in the morning, I try to do that.'

My eye caught these words in a newspaper. 'What a way to live!', I said to myself. Then I saw the writer's name; I had second thoughts. It was Laurens van der Post. He had been a farmer, a traveller, a soldier, a writer. He is a man of quiet faith. He has learned how to take life with a lighthearted confidence, and one day at a time; and this is how he saved the lives of thousands in a Japanese prisoner-of-war camp in Java.

A world of uncertainty – there is nowhere else you and I can make our life journey; and it is there that confidence can grow out of love, and love in my experience out of prayer.

I do not mean only 'saying prayers'. Prayer for me is whenever two great mysteries really meet – the supreme mystery who is God and that wonderful mystery who is you. I will try to spell this out in practical terms.

I have discovered all this in my journeys as a priest – and in the lives and writings of many whom I have met, not all of them by any means firm believers. I am grateful to them. Together we still have a long way to go. I wish you could join us in our venture of discovery.

Easter 1986   MARK GIBBARD
Oxford

PART ONE

THE REAL JOURNEY

1

Travelling Confidently in the World

I met her once, and only for a few hours, twenty years ago. But I shall never forget her – and her large, shining eyes, which seemed to welcome and really understand you. She had more than personal charm. Her friends called her *éblouie de Dieu*; for her radiance had something about it which I can only call supernatural.

Yet she was quite ordinary. Madeleine Delbrêl was the only child of a railway worker. She was a lapsed Catholic and called herself an atheist. In her teens her father's work brought them to Paris. She went to art galleries and to concerts. She tried to write poetry.

Then, as she said, she 'worked things out for herself' and came back to faith in God. She began to try to pray, at first like some of us, tentatively. Before long she could write, 'In reading and reflecting I have found God, but in praying I believe God *found me*.'

Yet all did not go smoothly for her. She became engaged to a Catholic, but it was broken off. Next she wanted to become a Carmelite nun; and that plan she gave up so as to take care of her parents. For thirty years, until they died, she supported them both.

During this time she became a social worker in the arrondissement of Ivry, dominated by the Communists in the Popular Front; she called Ivry 'my school of applied faith'. She lived in the narrow, grim Rue Respail. I visited the house after her death. I opened the heavy forbidding door, which made it look like a small factory. But inside, you at once felt you were in a warm, welcoming home; and there was a long narrow garden with outhouses which often sheltered refugees.

The telephone was always ringing. People kept coming and going all day and sometimes late at night too. There she lived, slim, agile, with an air of decision and energy – and with this unfailing radiance, *rayonnement*. Under all these pressures she retained her deep, joyful confidence in God.

For Madeleine and her friends this confidence came through prayer that was real. They had no oratory in that busy house; they could keep no strict timetable of prayer. But, as she said herself, prayer is whenever you really 'meet with the living God, the living Christ.'

Pressures and problems of life today

How often I remember Madeleine, when I meet in my journeys so many people with similar problems. They often share confidences with me during Bible-courses, retreats and workshops on prayer. Students sometimes say, 'How can I prevent all these worries about exams and grants, interviews and personal tangles from getting on top of me? And in the end I may not get a job.' Also in our competitive world, men and women ask me, 'How can I cope with all this stress?' 'How can I manage these difficult family and personal problems of mine?' 'How can I deal with my depressions and other troubles that come out of my past unhappy experiences? I feel so lonely and empty.' And how can any of us not be worried with all the anxieties of this nuclear age?

I realize these questions are more difficult for sensitive people. But it is not only a matter of temperament. It is even more finding out how to live on inner personal resources. You and I want to face our problems – not to evade them. We don't want to be like the man who said to God, 'These problems are too much for me, Lord; stop the world going round so fast; I want to get off.'

Confidence in God in New Testament times

In contrast to this I would like to quote a friend I have

never met. Yet from his letters I think I know him better than some people I see daily. In some points he is a man of his own times – and aren't we nearly all? – but the deep principles of his life are always worth weighing up.

He is Paul the apostle, a person of confidence and courage, like Madeleine; he is living under even greater strain. He is first having to tackle the personal tensions in the Christian communities; so he speaks of 'the daily pressure of my anxiety for all the churches'. But even more he feels, as most people of his day did, the threat of massive demonic powers. They are very real to him; he calls them 'principalities and powers' and 'world rulers of this present darkness'.

This is why Paul would understand us and our anxieties today. We too have first our personal worries. But like him we also feel threatened by almost uncontrollable economic and social forces. These are producing in many places unemployment, racial hostility, violence, terrorism and the spread of atomic weapons. Much of our reaction to them wells up from depths of our personal and collective unconscious.

Paul is writing about this tough journey of ours through life and death – not as a theologian in a library, but as a man always on the move amongst, he tells us, 'dangers in the city, dangers at sea, dangers among false brethren'. Yet he can say, 'I am persuaded' – and his precise word means that he has come to this faith not all in one leap, but by gradually growing into this confident certainty.

> For I am persuaded that neither death, nor life, nor angels, nor principalities, nor things present, nor things to come, nor powers, nor height, nor depth, nor anything else in all creation, will be able to separate us from the love of God in Christ Jesus our Lord.

'The love of God in Christ Jesus'; Paul says love

immense and unchangeable, is always there, always with us. This is where our confidence springs from.

God's love grasped now
God's love is there, objectively there. How can we grasp it now? By thinking, by meditating and by loving one another.

First, by thinking. Let me speak personally. I was brought up a Christian. At the university I became an agnostic. I had to work my way back with my mind, as Madeleine did. Thinking took time, as I will explain later. I still had my difficulties. I know I may yet have dark patches to come. But I am now, to use Paul's word, 'persuaded' that God's love is objectively there and is reliably revealed in Christ Jesus.

Secondly, by meditating. Thinking alone did not give me enough motivation. I needed also to meditate, to accept God and his love with heart as well as mind. This meditating I am going to spell out later as 'prayer with a heart open to God'.

Thirdly, by loving one another. God's love is objective; its reality does not depend upon the ups and downs of human experiences. Yet I have found that the experience of what human friendship and love is helps us to grasp more firmly God's love and to bring it into our lives.

Yet some people tell me that what I write about God's love does not 'speak' to them – often because of painful experiences in their families, in friendships and in love. I understand this from many conversations with others and from some experiences of my own. But let me assure you that I have met men and women who found it hard to begin to believe and have had sad experiences of human love and yet have come through to a firm, personal grasp of God's ever-present love for them. For neither can *our* past separate us from the love of God.

So it is through thinking and meditating and through fellowship with one another that we can grasp steadily the reality of God's love. We can then live in the confidence that in God there is a power of love sufficient for all the needs of our journey and of our service in today's world.

Our faith renewed

Now I should be untrue to myself and to my own experience, if I tried to persuade you that anyone can acquire and live in this faith by one decisive turning to God. The word Paul uses, as we have seen, means that he *grew* into this confident faith. Rudolf Bultmann, the New Testament scholar, has said, 'The decision of faith is never final, it needs *constant renewal in every situation.*'

There are many people who have wanted to believe but have never been able to be quite sure of God. I would like them to find in the perspective of that statement – and of this book – a new angle of approach. For in each new day, in each new situation there is a chance to reach out for a *fresh* approach to God.

On the other hand this scholar's statement may perhaps sound too vague for those Christians to whom God has already made himself vividly real on some particular day. I understand their feelings; for God made himself real to me on a particular day in a retreat, when I was a young graduate.

Yet I still stand by that statement. We shall need to keep it in mind and heart, I think, through all the changes of life's journey. In particular we shall need it in our praying. Prayer, real prayer, is much more than a regular self-discipline. It is a personal venture – a venture that needs renewal frequently, the re-affirmation and the re-expression of its inner reality.

If this does not seem clear about praying, perhaps we can see it in an experience more familiar to many men and women. When two people have come to a deep love and perhaps have enjoyed for years a real marriage partnership, they still know that they *cannot take their love for granted*, they can't assume that once they are committed or once they are married, all that really matters has been settled. On the contrary, they know they need to say and to hear genuinely said, 'I love you'. However deep, however longstanding their love, they know they need in a variety of ways to express it; and each time their love is genuinely expressed it is deepened and made more secure.

So with prayer that is real. It is, like love, a venture ever to be re-affirmed, re-expressed, and ever deepened.

The needs of others and their service
I have become convinced that we all need deep down the divine friendship as much as we need human companionship. Further this divine friendship can then bring more sensitivity and strength into all our caring for others. Yet many people, often kind and gifted, do not know what they themselves are missing; and they do not see how much more they might be giving to others, if only they had this divine friendship. How can you and I help them – and help them to give more to others? We can only share with them what we ourselves deeply possess.

I remember talking about this with a well-travelled American friend of mine, Father Basil Pennington. We were sitting in his small office in the Cistercian monastery at Western in Massachusetts. He made two striking observations. 'The man or woman whose love of God has matured through years of intimacy is the one', he said, 'whose presence brings to others unfolding love.' I have known some people like that. Perhaps you have too. What a strength they are to us. I remember he also said, 'There is no greater resource we can give people than to open to them the way by which they can come to experience most intimately and constantly how much they are loved by God.'

To be sure we are loved by God and to be able to help others to be sure – that is our vital, inner resource for the human journey and our service in the world.

8

Laurens van der Post, Madeleine Delbrêl and countless others have lived on that resource in our hard-headed and often violent world of today. This is what is going to count in our lives.

2

Personal Resources
for the Journey

'John, you're so desperately dependent on the approval of other priests and of the people of your parish', said his outspoken sister-in-law to Mgr John Farrell, the apparently successful priest in a thriving parish, 'so much so that at times you don't have any character at all of your own.'

In Andrew Greeley's novel *Lord of the Dance* John's family, poor Irish immigrants, had in two generations built up an engineering empire in Chicago. There were skeletons in the cupboard – dubious business deals and suspicions about how the ill-tempered head of the family came to fall down the stairs and crack his skull. There were now two sons; Roger, a well-established academic and a promising politician, something of a womanizer; and John, devoted to his vocation.

At forty-two he had the opportunities he wanted; an exciting and prosperous parish and a weekly TV chat show at a peak time. Relaxed and tactful, he interviewed actresses, feminists and liberals and explained to them the teaching of the Church. The programme was repeated on other channels.

Many of his fellow-priests became jealous. They started a whispering campaign; he had overdone things. Articles appeared in the press; Mgr Farrell was, they said, 'on an ego trip'; he was letting the standards of the Church down; 'Someone should stop him from this over-exposure to the media.' These comments began to split up his generally loyal and wealthy congregation. Divisions were polarized. In all this turmoil John feared that some of the shadier things in his family history might leak out.

Fear was undermining all his fine work. He could not face his family's past, accept himself, stand on his own feet, challenge his opponents and so mature into his true self and do the work he was called to do in Chicago.

The mystery of who we are
Authentic prayer happens, I have suggested, whenever the mystery of ourselves really meets with the supreme mystery who is God. By each of these mysteries I do not mean something vague, still less unreal; but something rich and profound, beyond all description.

To begin to grasp the wonderful mystery of ourselves we have to try to fulfil two conditions. We have both to accept ourselves as we are now, and also to be prepared to grow into our true selves. What makes these two conditions difficult for us, as for Mgr Farrell, is fear, lack of confidence. Yet without accepting these two conditions, we can neither deeply pray nor truly serve others.

Many people set out to serve others, but often fail for one of two apparently opposite reasons, though both really grow out of this inner fear.

On the one hand, some develop bossy ways. 'Come on', they say too heartily, 'it's quite clear. Do it this way; let's get on with it.' This method may either turn out robots or provoke resistance, active or sullen. This bossiness is a cover up for fear, like Mgr Farrell's fear of loss of his reputation.

At the other extreme, some soon lose the self-confidence they set out with. They become unduly diffident. They dither, don't give a clear lead and seem unable to share with others what they themselves have learned through their own experience and training.

We have just looked at two extremes. But how many there are right across the spectrum of service, who are handicapped, even haunted, by some kind of fear. I care for them so much, because I have experienced fear

11

in the journey of my own life. The answer to fear is confidence in God's love, love received through prayer.

But I must say something more about fear. Fear is not wholly a bad thing. Fear of disease leads us to take precautions. Fear of a fall keeps a climber from being foolhardy. Many people have the idea that others are far less afraid than they are. But all normal people are afraid. Lloyd George, orator as he was, still was so nervous before a great speech, that he went off his food for a day, so his daughter tells us. 'If people think they are exempt from fear,' wrote Paul Tournier, the Swiss doctor and psychiatrist, 'that is because they have repressed their fears. Fear is part of human nature.'

A very important thing in the journey of life for many people is to recognize and let go their old fears, old resentments and old conformities to what perhaps parents and other authoritarian figures expected of us. Only if we are courageous enough to say goodbye to all this, can we be born and grow into our new, at first unfamiliar, but true emerging selves. This is the mystery of who we really are.

So we gradually grow to feel sure of ourselves. I do not mean becoming opinionated and self-reliant. I mean being confident through a real relationship of love with God. William Temple spoke of this kind of confidence, 'If you are sure of yourself, you don't fear what is going to meet you round the next corner.'

Accepting who we are
When I reflect on the mystery of who we are, I sometimes say to a friend, 'I think I see three you's in you, and I appreciate each one of them.' I do not mean there are clear lines between them. I call them our external self, our present inner self and our emerging true self. I am not talking in psychological terms, although like many people today I have long taken an interest in psychology. I speak rather as a poet or as an understanding friend.

But before we consider these three selves, we need to see where we are now. We cannot become what we can become, unless we first accept ourselves, warts and gifts, as we are. We have to learn to forgive ourselves, just as God forgives us. We need to appreciate and love ourselves in the way God loves us. Jesus himself told us to love ourselves; he said we should love others, not instead of ourselves, but *as* we love ourselves.

I realize how difficult this is for some people. But I have seen many grow into a right love of themselves, once they have grasped that they are really, constantly loved by God. And God's love is real, objective, as we have seen, unforgettably revealed in Jesus Christ, in his words and life of love. This is a stupendous truth. I will try to show how we can make it part of our very selves. Let me repeat; we need to accept ourselves – and God's unchangeable love.

When we cannot accept ourselves, we have what people call today 'a low self-image'. The primary source of our troubles and anxiety is not our circumstances; it is our low self-image, the way we see ourselves.

Our exterior self
I would like first to say a little about our exterior self, the one we show to the world, the way we speak, the way we dress. Paul Tournier calls it *notre personnage*. In some circles people now talk of it disparagingly. 'Say what you think. Don't be a hypocrite', they tell us. 'Laugh loud, be angry and shout, anyway show how you are feeling.' If we did this, we might turn our homes, our colleges, our offices, our factories into beargardens. When I think of close friends of mine and of several men and women, who still influence me, I see how their exterior selves truly express what they are. In no way are their *personnages* polite, unconvincing facades. Our exterior selves, if sincere, can be useful; for it is through them that we begin to make and deepen our relationships.

13

In fact, we sometimes *need* an exterior self, which is distinct from our inner self. For we rightly cannot always wear our hearts on our sleeves. A surgeon in the operating theatre has to be almost as sterile as his instruments. Your bank manager, when discussing your overdraft, needs his kindly, professional manner, whatever his inner thoughts about you may be. These are two – admittedly extreme – instances.

But we should examine our *personnages* from time to time to see whether they are carrying out their proper function. We misuse them when we continue to keep them on with those close to us, and indeed with others, when it would be helpful to let them know something of our inner experience. Their misuse can be serious, when our *personnages* begin to be dishonest and insincere. They then become masks or even worse. 'If they are worn often and long enough', as his sister-in-law said of Mgr Farrell, 'masks become the person.'

Our present self
Before we examine our deep, emerging true self, let us look at our a-little-below-the-surface, present self. Every one of us is unique; and whatever I write is bound to be over-simplified. For all of us our present self is fundamentally good, because God created it. Yet through the history of our race and through our own experience our human nature has to some extent become warped. But in our life's journey it can through God's love and by prayer be brought into good order. So we can travel with confidence.

In our present self each of us has gifts, fears, wounds and instinctive drives. First, all around us are people finding in themselves gifts, a new joy in music, in painting, in photography or in do-it-yourself jobs. Sometimes it has been only a chance remark in the past that has shut off these pleasures from us. It was so with me. A games master, whom I rather admired as schoolboys do, said in a neat phrase, 'Men are concerned with

14

things, women with people; men with achievements, women with feelings.' The result was that art, music, poetry and real personal relationships were something of a closed book to me for years. I said I hadn't time for them. They were for girls and women. My scientific studies were my passion. And I am not the only man whose life has been narrowed. Perhaps women's interests and skills are sometimes narrowed in the opposite direction. All of us have gifts to discover within ourselves.

Next, in our present self, there are a variety of fears. They may not be the same as those of Mgr Farrell. But they are fears which make us anxious – fears about not getting a job and keeping it, about the health of someone on whom we very much depend, about the spread of violent thefts and terrorism, about nuclear bombs getting into irresponsible hands. Compared with us, other people often look so calm and secure. We feel inferior and ashamed of our fears. This is why it is good to find someone we can gradually and trustfully share our fears with. Then we discover others are as fearful and vulnerable as we are. This discovery is an emancipation. So we liberate one another. We accept ourselves and our fears. We go on in our journey of life, much relieved, more confident in God's love.

Then, there are also wounds and pains deep inside nearly all of us. They have come in such different ways. Perhaps at some time – maybe quite early in life – we have been subjected to sarcasm or to injustice or cruelty. Men and women are at times deeply hurt in a love relationship, or have been disillusioned in a marriage which at first looked so promising. Some of us, it is true, are tough, resilient men and women. Yet even so, these old wounds and resentments can secrete a kind of poison into the depths of our personalities. This is one reason why many people find it hard to cope with the inevitable pressures and problems of their life today; this poison saps their strength. We will see how we can find help in these inner troubles through friendship and real prayer.

Finally, there are powerful drives, which flow in what T. S. Eliot called 'the river within us', a river of immense vitality. Psychologists of various schools write about it; so do authors of modern books on Christian living and on praying. This life-giving river should make us in very varied ways men and women of creativity. This river within often runs steadily; sometimes it rushes on turbulently, at other times it is partly blocked with boulders and rubble. But it is still fundamentally good.

In this river there are various feelings of aggression. Sometimes these lead men and women to dominate others and to speak and act with violence. This is why many people try to clamp down these feelings, to forget them or else to disown them. But such a habit can cause depressions and other sad – and often apparently inexplicable – results. But on the other hand our aggressive feelings can be channelled constructively, like a mountain torrent which produces hydro-electric power for towns and irrigation water for farms. In fact these forces can give us courage to speak up for an unpopular cause and energy to tackle some long and demanding task. They can put some indispensable steel into us for life's struggles and responsibilities.

Running in this river is also our sexuality; and this too is fundamentally God-given, as all orthodox Christians believe officially. But powerful sexual impulses can cause so many tragedies. This is part of the reason why some, at least of older, people were brought up to regard them with suspicion and fear. So they have tried to force these feelings also underground and out of sight; and again often with unhappy results. Yet it is these same feelings which cause people to fall in love, to marry, to bring up children in an atmosphere of love, and to enrich with sensitivity their whole network of friendships and human relationships.

This acknowledging and truly accepting our gifts, our fears, our wounds and our drives is essential for real living with others. Only as we grasp and possess this turmoil within us, shall we be able really to understand others; if not, we shall probably only patronize them. This accepting ourselves is equally necessary for real praying. The anonymous author of a fourteenth-century treasure book on prayer, *The Cloud of Unknowing*, tells us 'to get a true knowing and feeling of yourself as you are'; then he adds, 'and you will soon get a true knowing and feeling of God as he is.' On a notice-board in a Welsh convent a card reads, 'We come to God either as we are, or not at all. Angry or anxious, adoring or bored, God accepts us as we are.'

Our true self
Our true self is the self that God means us to become. It is already beginning to emerge within us. God does not want us to be drilled into a standard type. He has made us – or rather is making our true selves – in a rich variety of men and women. I believe the book of Genesis gives us in a kind of poetic imagery insight into what he intends us to become. 'So God created man in his own image', it says, 'in the image of God he created him'; whatever else these words may mean, they speak of the link and the deep affinity there is between God and man. Though God is so great and we are so many and so small, yet we can have an intimate relationship with God analogous to human friendship and love. St Augustine, who did not live a sheltered life, put this truth into unforgettable words:

'God, you have made us for yourself;
and our hearts are restless until they rest in you.'

But immediately Genesis has said, 'in the image of God he created him', it adds in the same breath, 'male and female he made them.' God made them not only to

17

bring up a family. He made them for one another. The translation in the Authorized Version that Eve was to be Adam's 'helpmate' does not bring out the meaning of the Hebrew. It really means that she is his *vis-à-vis*, that is, reciprocally, his partner. God designed man and woman to be complementary, not only in a marriage partnership, but also in a wide variety of enriching human relationships. 'He who does not love', the first letter of John says, 'does not know God.' Our friendship with God is inextricably interwoven with our human loves, friendships and relationships. To love is sometimes difficult. In real love we set one another free to become our true selves.

We can begin only where we are. Then God will see that all that is good in our present self – and in our exterior self – will mature and be integrated into our emerging true self. This again is the mystery that is you.

Our journey and our maturity
Our journey of life is our service in the world. It is a journey we can make with joyful confidence because God's sustaining love is always with us. We have begun to see also that we have personal, inner resources enough for it. This journey is not just the passing of the years, like Shakespeare's Seven Ages of Man. It is a fascinating journey, in which we discover our real selves and so grow into our maturity.

St Paul saw it was his life task to bring everyone – not only an élite – to be *teleios en Christo*, 'mature in Christ'. This phrase was misleadingly translated in the Authorized Version of the Bible as 'perfect in Christ'; modern versions rightly translate it 'mature in Christ'. We are not angels. We are to help one another to grow not into the blameless perfection of angels, but into the maturity of men and women. This is a practical matter. For those who aim at being 'perfectionists' suffer from scrupulosity and many unnecessary anxieties.

18

Christians also realize that they cannot become mature by human resources alone. They see that for maturity they need God's love, which comes through Christ. This is why Paul writes not only of our becoming mature, but of our becoming 'mature in Christ'. Further, we grow to maturity, not alone, but together. We are like Chaucer's pilgrims – rather a mixed bag – on the road to Canterbury. That is why Paul also says that we grow not individually into mature men and women but together 'into mature manhood, into the fullness of the stature of Christ'. We grow out of individualism into a corporate oneness in Christ, into the Christ-that-is-yet-to-be.

Maturity is never – even with all God's help – our achievement in this life. It gives us our sense of direction. Those who try too hard seldom really succeed. We become too anxious. God expects us to grow towards maturity like the flowers. 'They toil not', Jesus said of them, 'neither do they spin.' Our garden flowers do not push themselves, they open themselves. Our growth is like theirs, I think – and in three ways.

Our own uniqueness
Each flower is different, and so are we. We are not supposed to model ourselves on others, however wonderful they may be. We are to unfold into our true selves. When Rabbi Eleazar died, God did not ask him why he had not become like Abraham the man of faith or like Moses the man of action; God quietly said, 'My son, why did you not become Rabbi Eleazar?'

We should never undervalue ourselves. 'The very hairs of your head', said Jesus, 'are all numbered'. We are each irreplaceably precious to God; and so should we be to ourselves. Each one of us, young or not so young, vigorous or handicapped, highly gifted or apparently ungifted, has hidden within us a particular beauty of personality. It is this that we are to discover and value. The chrysanthemum in its autumn glory

19

does not envy the snowdrop that greets the spring or the red rose of summer. How often have I heard it said in Germany, *Werde was du bist* – 'Become what you are'!

What I have just written is not contradicted by what Paul writes, 'Be imitators of me, as I am of Christ.' For Paul is not thinking of an external unimaginative imitation of Jesus, still less of rigid rules. Paul wishes us to enter into the inner spirit of Jesus. That is why he says, 'We have the mind of Christ' and 'Let this mind be in you which was also in Christ Jesus.' Possibly the title of the Christian classic, *The Imitation of Christ*, may in the past have been taken in too wooden a way. 'What would Jesus have done in my situation?' is not always a good question to put to yourself. For he was never in it. He saw the stars only with the eyes of a first-century man; he was never married, never had to face the problems of twentieth-century parents; he never had to decide his attitude to management or to trade unions. True he taught us about life; but what we most need in life is his openness to God and to one another; and this, we believe, God wishes us to cultivate through his Spirit.

Many of us find this openness difficult. We cling, as we have seen, to the past with its familiar securities, rather than stride out, confident in God, into the future – into the venture of maturing into our true selves. And today is the first day of the future.

Openness to others
The flowers grow into their own particular beauty because they are open to spring showers and the summer's early morning dew. We all need the sparkling water of human friendship and love; otherwise we only exist, we don't live and grow. 'To be alive', Eric Fromm, the psychiatrist, said, 'is to be loved.' Rightly we are individuals; but we cannot grow as individualists.

Warm, trustful friendships are so important for our journey into maturity. They can help us in at least three ways; they can show us those gifts now hidden in our present inner selves; they can gradually heal the wounds there; and they can also free us from the quirks and oddities which have built up inside us. How this happened to C. S. Lewis himself is pointed out by Humphrey Carpenter in his book *Inklings*, an appreciation of C. S. Lewis' circle of friends in Oxford. Lewis had lived for nearly sixty years as a bachelor and for most of that time as a well-known English literature don and a popular religious writer. He had almost inevitably acquired various donnish mannerisms and postures. Then surprisingly he fell in love with an outspoken American, Joy Davidman, married her and had a short wonderful marriage until she died from cancer. This partnership helped Lewis to discover his true self. 'His manner, all his postures which had brought him success, had hidden his inner nature', so Carpenter wrote, 'not merely from others, but from himself. It was only when his marriage somehow removed that veil that he found his true nature.'

I quite understand why many people hesitate to be drawn into such a deep and open relationship in friendship or even within marriage itself. It looks like giving up our independence. But it is not losing real independence, it is rather becoming realistic about ourselves and about life. A further problem is that to enter into such a relationship we have initially to accept one another as we are; and that may indeed be difficult. Yet, as Simone Weil said, 'If I do not love them as they are, it will not be they whom I love, and my love will be unreal.' But then gradually each helps the other to discover the full richness of their true selves. 'Jointly the two', wrote C. S. Lewis about his own marriage, 'become fully human.'

It is not only in good marriages that this can happen, but also through a wide variety of friendships and human relationships – each with its own level of engagement. We see Jesus loving everyone with a love appropriate to each – his mother, his disciples, his friends Mary, Martha and Lazarus, and those who turned to him for advice, forgiveness and healing. So we should try to appreciate all, and even care for those who grate on us; for sometimes a barbed word from them will, on reflection, show us something about our present selves of which we are only half-conscious. We see Jesus turning with love and forgiveness even to those who were crucifying him: 'Father, forgive them, for they do not know what they are doing.'

If we find it difficult to make real relationships with others, let us not be discouraged. The twelve disciples found it hard to get on with one another. There were plenty of tensions among the first Christians at Cornith. Our awkwardness with others we may put down to our shyness, our natural reserve, our early upbringing. We may honestly say this in explanation; but we shouldn't make it an excuse for not trying to grow into our true selves through our various relationships. And a way forward can often, as we will see later, be found through a genuine praying for others.

Openness to the Divine

Flowers need also the warmth of the sun. To grow into our true selves we need not only human friends, but also, I believe, some experience of the divine companionship and love. And here the human and the divine are often close to one another. Cardinal Basil Hume says, 'A parent's love or friendship or falling in love may enable us to explore more deeply the words "God is love".' Indeed sometimes human friendship and love can bring to us the divine love rather as our receiving the holy bread and wine brings to us our Lord's love in the sacrament of the eucharist.

For many people today our ability to be friends of God means next to nothing. But it is one of those gifts hidden in our inner selves. It is, I am convinced, an integral part of our being human. I understand how this capacity often remains undeveloped or has shrivelled up through an inadequate spiritual education or an unfavourable environment. Not only of our spiritual possibilities is this true, but also of our aesthetic capacities as well. Anyone, for example, who is brought up in a home or a school without music, is unlikely to discover his capacity for making and enjoying music. Something like this almost happened to Kathleen Ferrier. And what a loss it would have been, not only to her but also to thousands for whom her singing eventually brought such joy! She left school at fourteen and had an unsuccessful marriage. Although she was a fairly good pianist, her voice and gift for song went undiscovered until her late twenties. If on the other hand a few years earlier she had found happiness in marriage and home, she might have thought she already had everything that she needed – with not the slightest idea of her gift for song and its development. Luckily it was discovered.

In my journeys I have had the privilege of making friends with many wonderful men and women who have never discovered, or who have never developed, their capacity for the divine friendship. I can't help thinking how with that friendship they might have become even more wonderful people – and how much more they might then have enriched many others whose lives they touch.

I was once conducting a retreat for some French nuns. It was a silent retreat. Yet each afternoon we had a short time all together for what they called *échange*, so that they could, if they wished, give me some of their reflections. One afternoon I had said to them, rather as I have written in this chapter, what wonderful women they were, like the splendid flowers in their garden. 'We've never been told that before', replied one of the nuns. 'All the other priests have told us that we were

23

ordinary women with ordinary work to do and that we must not think too highly about ourselves.' I said to the nuns that this sort of self-depreciation sounded to me disastrous. The Sister Superior must have agreed with me. Our last silent meal together was a festal, candlelight meal. We had music, flowers on highly-polished tables and a little red wine. The Superior had written special verses on small cards and had put one at each place at table. There was one for me also; I could easily translate it, but its meaning did not dawn on me at once; it said, *Il est bon d'avoir quelqu'un qui cultive les fleurs* – 'It is good to have someone to cultivate the flowers.'

You and I, each of us, need someone to care for us like flowers. And we can be brought to an even deeper beauty by the Lord's own hand of love.

PART TWO

THE REAL GOD

3

Confidence in God

'I've been to church many times and heard many prayers, but none like this', wrote Fynn, an East-end worker between the wars, and at that time a bachelor. It was about a Cockney waif, Anna, whom he had befriended. He went on, 'I can't remember much about her prayer except it started off with "Dear Mister God, this is Anna speaking", and she went on in such a familiar way of talking to Mister God that I had the creepy feeling that if I dared to look behind me He would be there. I remember her saying, "Thank you for letting Fynn love me", and I remember being kissed goodnight, but how I got to bed I don't know.'

The book is based on fact. He only knew her for three and a half years. Before she was eight, she had an accident. With a smile on her face, she died saying, 'I bet Mister God lets me get into heaven for this.' Fynn added, 'And I bet he did too.'[1]

That is naïve, but it is real prayer. But can we sophisticated people of today with our knowledge of the universe around us and the inner world within us pray to God so directly, intimately, and with such a sense of reality? I have been gradually convinced that we can.

God the Supreme Mystery
Genuine prayer happens when the wonderful mystery who is the emerging you really meets with the supreme mystery of God. He is indeed beyond all we could say or imagine. We always come to him with a sense of

---

[1] From *Mister God, this is Anna*, published by Collins, 1974.

wonder. Yet he has disclosed to us the heart of that supreme mystery in the love we see in Jesus Christ. I will soon try to give you my reasons for saying this.

Whenever we pray, I am now persuaded, God knows and *does* something, not always what we ask. Because he is the ever-present love we see in Jesus, he cannot remain passive and unresponsive when we come to him. Further his love, like all true love, cannot be vague; it must be focused on individuals. How God responds to our prayers we cannot expect to understand, although I make a speculation about it in chapter seven. Anyway, there is also much that we enjoy in everyday life without knowing how it works. Paul reminds us that God 'is able to do so much more than we can ever ask for, or even think of'. For me all this is an integral part of my confidence in God and his love.

I realize that this belief in a God of love is dismissed by some modern people as incredible. Others would like to believe, but have never honestly been able to do so. And others used to believe it, but their belief has been gradually eaten away – how well I understand this – by the scepticism of our times; for others' doubts or half-doubts easily rub off on to us. There are also some Christians who accept it rather superficially; they might say, 'Yes, I agree'; but they have not yet been able to grasp it in mind and heart and make it 'part of themselves'. I will try to remain sensitive to each of these kinds of people.

In this chapter we are considering 'Why believe in God?' and 'What kind of God is the real God?' We will look at these questions chiefly from an intellectual angle; though, for me and for the New Testament, belief involves not only our intellects but also our hearts; it requires honest thinking, and some kind of meditating as well.

Why believe in God?
As I have said, I have been an agnostic myself. At the

28

university I lost all faith in God through a misunderstanding of psychology. I came to think that any idea of God was a projection, an illusion, like a mirage in the desert. In fact I became rather an aggressive agnostic. Then gradually – I do not quite know how it began – I felt that honesty required that I should think it over again, as Madeleine Delbrêl did. I was greatly helped by a priest-friend in Cambridge, who spent hours and hours talking these things over with me. Then the turning-point came quietly through the experience of my first retreat, although I went to it rather reluctantly through the persuasion of another friend. That, of course, was only a beginning; and since then I have had a long though stimulating journey to make, and I still have many miles to go.

It has been, I think, a reasonable journey, though I have sometimes had to take a step beyond the limits of reason, yet in the same direction. My search has shown me that there are at least three signposts to consider, pointing in the direction of God – first, our observations in the world of nature; secondly, the existence of ethical insights in our human experience; and, thirdly, widespread spiritual experience, by which I do not mean primarily visions or exceptional happenings, but a sense of God's presence and power gradually shaping our lives. I do not wish to write of these signposts in any more detail here, as I have devoted a chapter to them in my recent book, *Jesus, Liberation and Love*. The subject is dealt with far more adequately by Bishop Hugh Montefiore in his book, *The Probability of God* (SCM Press, 1985). Incidentally he shows how much smaller the gap is between many scientists and theologians than it was fifty or even twenty years ago.

These three signposts will not in themselves bring us to God, still less will they put pressure on us. They invite us to reflect carefully, and then decide. At first it may have to be a provisional decision; our honesty may require that. Isn't this how we mature in many other areas of our lives? Isn't this how many friendships are made? We first find an interest in one another, then we meet and talk and think; and, though emotions are also involved, we still need eventually to make our decision, a venture.

Some people, so it seems to me, often do not think hard enough either definitely to believe – or to disbelieve. An Anglican churchwarden, who had been to church for many years, went to a course on 'Christianity in the Twentieth Century'. During a discussion he in an unthinking but self-disclosing moment blurted out, 'I've never discovered who God is'. Then, surprised at what he had just admitted, he added, 'That's the first time I've ever dared to say that.' It was just then that for him the conference came alive, 'things began to happen', and his belief in God took on a new reality.

This thinking about God and so deepening our confidence in him is part of our intellectual search. But *this growing confidence in God is also fundamental for our human maturity.* We need warm, human relationships, as we have seen, so as to mature into our true selves. But we also need – let me repeat it – a similar relationship of confidence in God. I learned much about this from Alan Ecclestone in a retreat he conducted for our community. He was a priest in an industrial parish, a university lecturer in English literature and a man deep in politics. He has written, 'If we are not *growing* in prayer, we are not becoming mature human beings. We are leaving something undeveloped. God-given potentialities are being wasted.'

What kind of God? – God infinite, not remote, nor impersonal
When asked how to pray, Janet Stuart replied, 'Think glorious thoughts of God.' She travelled the world to visit the houses of her community. Yet she made you feel that you were the one person she really wanted to

see. So many people said this about her. Her humanness sprang, no one doubted, from her life of confident
prayer. What prevents many people from growing in
prayer and so in this humanness is not, as we often say,
lack of time; it is rather inadequate ideas of God. We
think narrow thoughts of God. Yet he is the supreme
mystery beyond all our words and thoughts.

Modern science takes away our breath by its disclosure of the immense size and age of the universe.
This vastness should give us a sense of wonder at the infinite greatness and glory of God. Yet it must not make
God seem remote, beyond us, like a cool, 'celestial
mathematician', as Sir James Jeans called him. For the
same natural science which shows us God's creative
power in the giant nebulae, shows it also in the unfolding life of his tiniest creature. I feel this deeply myself,
and I began my university studies in natural science. A
Hebrew poet holds these two truths together:

For thus says the high and lofty One
    who inhabits eternity, whose name is holy:
I dwell in the high and holy place
    and also with him who is of a contrite and
        humble spirit.

It is this balance of truths which should lead us into true
belief and prayer.

We should not make the mistake, as some do, of
thinking of God only as an immense impersonal force
behind the whole of creation and its evolution. It seems
to me – even apart from all we can learn from Jesus
Christ and in the scriptures – that, if God has brought
into existence personal beings like ourselves, then he
himself cannot be less complex, less wonderful, than we
his creatures are; that is, he cannot be impersonal, less
than personal; in fact we may be led eventually to think
of him as super-personal. Yet when we say he is personal, we do not picture him as a magnified man. We

31

mean rather that he can build up truly personal relationships with us. This personal language in prayer is very precious to us. But our closeness to God is, as we progressively discover, like the closeness of human affection, too deep for any words.

If we are going to grow in prayer, we need step by step to accept these truths, not with our intellects only, but with the whole of ourselves. A fellow-scholar used to go into a small Catholic church with Baron von Hügel, philosopher and man of prayer, on their way home from walks on Hampstead Heath, and he wrote of him, 'If you've never seen the massive head of the Baron bowed in adoration, you haven't seen half the man.'

God, caring for justice, yet not severe
So one mistaken idea of God, which puts people off from deeper prayer, is that he is remote and impersonal. The other distorted idea is that he is severe and legalistic.

Let us try to see how this idea of a severe God has arisen. God is concerned, not only with our personal relationships with him; he is concerned with the whole human family. He desires justice, fair dealing and brotherliness everywhere. In this universal purpose he uses us. This is clear from God's message both through the prophetic Hebrew leaders in the Old Testament and also through Jesus' emphasis on the rule of God on earth.

So God has given us guidelines for our collaboration with him in the affairs of the world. Yet again and again people have distorted these guidelines into a code of inflexible regulations. Jesus himself protested against this distortion. 'The sabbath', he said, as an example, 'was made for man, not man for the sabbath.' Jesus means that the Jewish law of the sabbath – and other regulations too – were intended by God to be blessings for man's good, for his health and well-being, and not heavy

32

burdens grudgingly borne on life's journey. Yet in contrast to this, God has even come to be regarded as an exacting master, ready to pounce on us for any deviations from these regulations, or even as a banker with a ledger of our debts and credits in his hand. So, in spite of all both Jesus and Paul have said against it, there has grown up a legalism among protestants as well as catholics.

This idea of God as a severe God blocks the building up of a constant, confident bond of love with him through prayer. Some people of the older generation were brought up with this severe, legalistic idea of God. Even if they have now rejected it with the tops of their heads, this distorted idea of God has often remained deep within them. So, when some disaster strikes them, they cry out spontaneously in distress, 'What have I done to deserve this?' The idea of a severe God is still there.

The effect of this legalistic severity is illustrated in an amusing story which Cardinal Basil Hume told about himself. He had been invited to speak to the Roman Catholic bishops in the United States about Vatican II's criticism of legalism. He explained how he had been brought up by a good, but severe mother. 'If I see you, my son,' she said to him, 'stealing an apple from my pantry, I'll punish you.' Then she added, 'If you steal an apple and I don't see you, Almighty God will see you and he will punish you.' The cardinal said that it had taken him years to realize that God might have said to him, 'My son, why don't you take two?'

If we wish to know what the *real* God, who longs for our friendship, is like, let us look primarily not at the stars, nor at any code of regulations, but at Jesus.

The real God disclosed in Jesus

'He who has seen me has seen the Father' says St John's gospel. In that verse is crystallized what the New Testament says about God's revealing himself to us in Jesus.

33

Bishop Stephen Neill says of it, 'The greater part of Christian theology has been unwilling to take this tremendous affirmation as seriously as it is taken in the New Testament'; and he adds:

> If when we see Jesus Christ we see God, then any previous idea we may have had of God must undergo a reconstruction which amounts to a re-building from the basement to the coping stone.

It incidentally involves, I think, an equally drastic change in what we mean by prayer.

This statement about Jesus Christ is not just theological speculation; what lies behind it goes back, I believe, to the lips of Jesus himself. I have spent a good deal of my life lecturing about this. I could say very much more. Briefly, it seems to me that Jesus was usually reticent in speaking about himself; and this makes even more impressive what he does say.

In a parable Jesus compared God to a landowner, who sent servants to collect the grape harvest. The workers on the estate ill-treated these servants and sent them back. The owner then said, 'I will send no more servants; instead I will send my only son; they are bound to respect him.' Yet in fact the workmen turned the son out of the vineyard and killed him. The meaning of Jesus' story was clear to his friends. The servants were the great Hebrew prophets, whom God had earlier sent to his people. The son was obviously Jesus himself, and it was clear that he was not one more highly-inspired human teacher; but that he was in quite a different category, man-one-with-God in a deeply unique way. This meaning was equally clear to his opponents, who at once stepped up their plot to have Jesus executed for blasphemy.

It is from such statements of Jesus that we accept the truth that he, through his unique closeness to the Father, can really disclose to us God, his love, and his offer to us of so close a relationship through prayer. 'He who has seen me has seen the Father'. This is what makes me eager and confident to come to God in all my praying and living.

The implications for us of Jesus' oneness-with-God
Whenever we see Jesus in the gospels going out in love to every kind of person in every kind of mood, we are seeing disclosed God's love for us today in every circumstance – in our joys, in our bewilderments and our depressions.

We watch Jesus enjoying himself at the wedding party. Then the wine begins to run out. How embarrassed the bridegroom and the guests are. Jesus hears about this through his mother. He provides more wine. Today, as then, Jesus doubles our joys, as we turn to him in prayer.

The blind beggar, Bartimaeus, was coming to ask Jesus for his help, but he could not get near him because of the crowd. He tried shouting out to attract Jesus' attention. People told him to be quiet. Bartimaeus was close to Jesus, yet felt so far from him. He was frustrated and bewildered. Then Jesus, ever sensitive, heard the blind man and called him; and through the man's faith healed him. And Jesus is alert to our every need.

There come to nearly all of us, to some of us more than others, times of depression and despair. There was a paralysed man who for thirty-eight years had sat by the pool of Bethesda in Jerusalem. He believed that if he could be the first to get into this pool when its water bubbled up, he would be healed. Day by day all those years he had been carried and put there by the pool. But nothing had happened for him. He was in the depths of despair. One day Jesus came and said to him, 'Do you really want to be healed?' Then Jesus told him, 'Take up your stretcher and walk.' However discouraged we may feel, we can turn to Jesus, to one who appreciates us and understands. Indeed he understands our troubles from within. He can sympathize with us, for he too has suffered.

In our every experience of joy and of trouble he comes near to us with understanding. In his love and wisdom he doesn't always give us what we ask. Paul asked him to take away his 'thorn in the flesh', which may have been some serious trouble with his eyes or perhaps epilepsy. But the Lord said, 'No; you must learn to live with it, Paul; but my grace will be sufficient for you.' In the same way God does not always take away our troubles, but he stays beside us in constant companionship; and we discover, like Paul, that God's grace and love are sufficient for our needs.

So because we see in Jesus and his love the Father and his ever-present love, we can, whatever our situation may be, come to God in Christ – and come in confidence.

Our participation in Jesus' confidence in the Father in daily life
More needs to be said about this. Jesus spoke simply to God in Aramaic as *Abba*, 'my own dear Father', in contrast to the elaborate prayer-language of the devout Jews of his time. Professor Jeremias, who has examined their prayers minutely, has said, 'It was something new, something unique and unheard of, that Jesus dared to take this step and to speak with God as a child speaks with his father, simply, intimately, securely.' In Gethsemane Jesus prayed 'Abba'. It was in this intimate confidence in his Father that he found strength for all his immense life work right to the very end.

Extraordinary as it may seem, God means us, ordinary men and women, to participate even in Jesus' own confidence in the Father. This is how Jesus himself puts it in the gospel; he says, 'No one knows the Son except the Father; and no one knows the Father except the Son – and anyone to whom the Son chooses to reveal him.' The word 'know' here means to know in its deepest sense, 'to know through loving'. So no one can know and love the Son in this way but the Father alone; and, as we should expect, no one can know and love the Father in this way but the Son alone. Then Jesus adds these quite unexpected words, 'and also any to whom the Son chooses to reveal the Father'. So Jesus tells us that people can actually share in his *own* knowing, loving and confidently trusting the Father. These people – as Jesus' preceding words show – are not the wise and sophisticated, but 'babes', namely, the humble, ordinary followers of Jesus. That is to say, *you and I can share in Jesus' own confidence in the Father* in our daily praying and living.

Yet there are people, I know, who perhaps because of unhappy relations with their own fathers, find it difficult to speak to God as 'Father'. They need not worry about this. For in the scriptures God is also spoken of as friend or even as beloved; and God's love is compared as well to a mother's love. We can speak to God in whichever word we prefer. The word does not matter much. What does matter is the fact of God's love for us. 'And *nothing* can separate us from the love of God in Christ Jesus.'

To come to God with confidence in this whole-hearted way is never our achievement. It does not depend on any special skills or efforts of ours, but on our being open to the Spirit, who can work within us. *Confidence is a God-given ability, through the Spirit.* Paul always encourages us to live and to pray trusting in God. And he tells us *how* it can be, for he says, 'God has sent the Spirit of his Son into our hearts, through whom we can say Abba, Father.' He means that you and I can speak to God as *Abba*, and live in Christ's own confidence in his Father, just because the Spirit of Jesus dwells in our hearts; as he has dwelt in the hearts of men and women of prayer across the centuries.

4

Doubts and Difficulties

Janet Baker has given us in her charming book, *Full Circle*, the diary of her last year as an opera singer. 'The question, "Are you religious?"', she tells us, 'was flung towards me like a bucket of ice-cold water in almost every interview I've ever given.' As she answered it the problem also of catastrophes and personal suffering always cropped up. She wrote of it and of her modest faith:

> The terror, the destruction, which occurs in nature, is enough to turn many people away from the idea of a loving Father completely. The problems of suffering, pain and evil surround us, for which an explanation may never be given. Nevertheless I choose to believe that behind it all is a sense of order, of purpose and finally of Love.

The problem cannot be dodged. Unless we face it, we cannot trust, we cannot pray. We may never find, as Dame Janet says, a logical explanation of it; but we all need insight and strength to cope with it – and to help others to cope with it.

A first step towards helping

I would like to show that suffering need not stop us trusting God and praying genuinely. I will try to write in a practical way. All the time I shall be feeling with you the tragedy and burden of this problem. Let us be realistic, not pessimistic. Suffering is for each one of us inevitable. 'Man is born to trouble, as the sparks fly upward.' So let us, as far as we can, be prepared and not be caught off our guard. Eventually we may manage – through God's strengthening love – even 'to rejoice in our sufferings', as Paul says. That is a long journey. Yet men and women of faith and prayer have done it. Suffering, far from weakening our trusting and praying, can in the long run strengthen them.

When suffering first strikes us or our neighbours, the immediate and deepest need is love – love which shows itself in understanding, support and practical help. We must try to go along beside the sufferer in genuine sympathy and prayer. Prayer will express itself in a different way each time. It will be trustful prayer, but sometimes silent and hidden prayer. Only when the first shock has been met are words of advice, encouragement and explanation normally useful. Even then there are no pat answers which we can learn in advance.

We may remember how in our own troubles we've said to ourselves, 'I'll talk to So-and-so; he's been through it; he'll understand.' So when we are helping others, we may be able at the *right* moment to say, 'Try now to accept your sufferings positively. In this way you can prepare yourself to understand and so to love other sufferers who in the future may turn to you for help.' Our sufferings can become our path towards loving others. We can heal the inner wounds of others, only because we are, as Henri Nouwen, a Roman Catholic priest says, ourselves 'wounded healers'.

Facing the unfairness of life
We are – or at least we wish to grow into – men and women of trust in God. This means that we must face with open eyes the unfairness of life. Why do comparatively innocent people have to suffer so much? Why do so many evil or careless people 'get away with it', as we say? The problem of Job will never be *logically* answered. And sufferings are often on such a massive scale.

Sufferings are unfairly distributed – but so also are physical strength, intellectual ability and artistic skills! I cannot believe that God – because he is the God of love revealed in Jesus – *sends* earthquakes or famine or disease. These things are the working out of those natural sequences, which scientists observe and record. God does not normally suspend these sequences to prevent trouble. If I may strike a lighter note for a moment and not be considered too flippant: if God sometimes intervened to suspend the law of gravity, we should have some strange games of football. This is the kind of world in which we have to live. To try to cope with its sufferings is one of the signs of our maturity. I hope I do not sound unfeeling.

God wishes us to grow into our human maturity and also into our full use of scientific research and skills so as to foresee and prevent catastrophes as far as we can, and to meet tragic situations with rapid and brotherly care. This is one of the ways in which we learn and practise being 'members one of another'.

Nor can I use my belief in the life to come as a way of making up for all the evils and the unfairness of this world. Quite the contrary. I regard this life – although very important in itself – as preparation and training for the next life. This is why the life to come makes me not less but more concerned about housing and education, justice and fairness in this life. Yet on one particular point the future life gives me encouragement and solid hope. When a small child or young person dies tragically, I am sure that this is not the end, but rather that this young life will in the future blossom and develop in the immediate presence of God.

Light through the clouds now
Yet in spite of all that I have just written, I must admit that there are still for me – and I expect for some of you – days when life is black. Sometimes life is like the sky covered by heavy clouds, clouds of natural disasters,

clouds of anxiety and depression in our own lives. It would be dishonest of us to try to minimize or try to explain away these black clouds.

But for those of us who can take the New Testament into our hands, there is always a beam of sunlight, perhaps faint, piercing those clouds. This beâm of light, which I can see even on my darkest days, is the daily life of Jesus in the gospels. In him we see love always going out to every kind of person in every situation. In fact his never-failing love is the revelation of God's unchangeable love for us. When we watch Jesus and his love then, we are seeing God and his love for us today. 'He who has seen me has seen the Father.' I cannot tell you how much those words have steadied me on my black days.

I think I can honestly say that what keeps me going in my praying, my travelling, my writing, my vocation – in spite of all the sufferings, pressures and frustrations – is this love of God disclosed in Jesus, then brought to me specially in the eucharist – and conveyed also to me through the caring of my friends.

I would like to say with Paul 'Christ's love for us directs us'. It strengthens me to face difficulties. I keep at it. Like you, I wish I could do better. I sometimes go on a bit grimly. Perhaps one day I shall be able, like Paul, 'to rejoice in my sufferings'.

Handling our sufferings positively
Paul could do this, because, so he tells us himself, he had learned how through his sufferings he could help 'to complete what still remains of Christ's sufferings on behalf of his body, the church'. He had discovered how he could make his sufferings, as well as his prayers, a channel through which Christ's liberating love can flow to others.

Of course Christ's life of love, which reached its climax in his dying and rising again for us, is enough to bring to the world his forgiveness, his liberating power

41

and all we need. But when we pray, God enables us to focus these blessings, to beam his love on to others. Yet our words of prayer would be shallow, unless we were at the same moment trying to give our *whole* lives to God for him to use to convey his love. Our lives include our sufferings. So we try to handle them positively, to offer them to God and to rejoice that God uses them for the good of those we care and pray for. Yet we can do this only through living close to, indeed *in*, the Lord.

We see this happening in the lives of men and women of prayer. Elizabeth Arrighi, an elegant Parisienne, married Felix Leseur, a doctor-turned-journalist. Soon after their honeymoon she developed an ulcer, which gave her pain for the rest of her life. More serious, a rift came between them. She remained a devout Catholic; he became a militant anti-clerical and atheist. She was always a charming hostess, though many of their guests were scoffing free-thinkers. For years she confided her suffering only to her confessor and to her personal journal. She prayed continually, 'Father, I offer up this pain and this loneliness along with the perfect offering of Jesus. Make of it all a living prayer for my beloved husband.' In her last months she began to see some change in him. 'Suffering that is accepted and offered up is the best of prayers', she wrote. Not long after her death, he tried to pray and then asked for Christian instruction – and eventually he gave himself to God and his service as a Dominican priest. We may feel that this wonderful way of prayer is at least for the present beyond us. But it points one of the ways ahead.

Co-existence of confidence with difficulties and doubts
I must confess it is at present beyond me. In my life confidence co-exists with difficulties and doubts. I love mountains and this helps me to see how to deal with clouds and doubts, which still come. It is a joy to admire the mountains and the far distances on a sunny cloudless day. But to me those are not the most

fascinating days among the mountains, but rather those other days when you can see patches of sunshine and shadow chasing one another across the successive lines of hills and mountains; and without clouds we cannot have these swift-moving areas of shadow. Clouds have their place in our mountain experiences. Lovers of mountains love them in all weathers.

All men and women of prayer have known doubt and darkness. Paul could write out of his own experience of darkness and frustration, 'In everything God works for good with those who love him'. God did not send the 'thorn in the flesh' and other hardships to Paul, but God used them to shape and mould Paul to become his true apostle. This was true even of Jesus as well. God used every experience Jesus went through – from his being loved as a baby by Mary and his hilarity at the wedding party at Cana, even to the darkness of Gethsemane and the cross – to shape Jesus and make him into the Liberator whom we so love.

God in his love is with us too in every situation. God never leaves us alone, isolated. His hand is always upon us like the potter with his hand on the clay. Out of a lump of clay the divine potter is trying to shape us into a beautiful vase. For this we should always be thanking God. Let us, as Paul says, give thanks 'in all circumstances, for this is the will of God in Christ Jesus for us.' We must respond to the various pressures of his skilled, loving fingers – and also of his thumb, working from within us.

5

God Within

At last after all those years I was there in the small remote town of Pokhara at the foot of the Himalayas in the heart of Nepal. Several times I had been to India and the East. Now I was again on my way back to England after lecturing and giving retreats in Kerala, Calcutta and the University of Serampore. Through a mutual friend some Jesuits invited me to Kathmandu, the capital, where they run two schools. They kindly arranged for me to visit Pokhara. On the afternoon of my arrival the mountains were to my disappointment hidden in cloud. So I went for a walk and took a boat to a Buddhist temple on a tiny island in a lake, Phewa Tal, indescribably peaceful. Then at the setting of the sun the clouds began to unfold. I was staying at a small hotel managed by a Tibetan family. After dinner I went on to the flat roof and saw the high mountains in the silvery gleam of the moon. The next morning I was up by 5.30, the birds were singing, the stars shining, the eastern sky was a pale yellow, then the rays of the rising sun caught in turn the seven snow-peaks of the Annapurna range, dominated by the 25,000-foot giant, Machhapuchhare, looking like a super-Matterhorn.

I now understood what drew several of my student friends in the '60s to make their way overland to Nepal – the majesty of the Himalayas, the Nepalese lifestyle and its serenity. Some of them had, it was true, bad experiences with drugs. Among them was an Oxford undergraduate whom I knew very well. He was a serious seeker. He said he could find no guru in Oxford – not among all the priests and ministers there! He

said – of course he may have misunderstood them –
they all talked about God as if he were a feudal
monarch. He wanted something deeper, something
within. He was extremist and rash, but he intended to
make a venture in prayer. There are plenty of others I
meet in our conventional West who also regard God
rather as a feudal monarch. He expects them, so they
think, to spend time in prayer and worship; which they
do grudgingly; or else neglect to do and so feel guilty
about it. Naturally they have little desire to go more
deeply into prayer.

But the God that is real we find is also God within us.

East and West
There is deeply rooted in our Christian tradition of
theology and prayer the truth that God is within us as
well as above us, God immanent as well as transcen-
dent. Much of this has been neglected in conventional
teaching in the Christian West. It always has been and
has remained strong in much oriental spirituality. John
Dunne, professor first at Yale and now at Notre Dame
University, has said in his book, *The Way of all the
Earth*, that many have had to journey, literally or
spiritually, to the East for their eyes to be opened.
Then on their return they can appreciate the spiritual
storehouse which we have always had – though often
unrecognized – in the Christian West.

Some of those who in recent years have helped us to
make this re-discovery in the West have themselves
been enriched by their contact with the East. Thomas
Merton was a typically secular man of this century. He
became a Trappist and began a deep study of traditional Christian spirituality. Next he corresponded with
Zen and Buddhist scholars. Finally he was allowed by
his abbot to go to India and Sri Lanka. On his way back
he was accidentally killed by an electric shock at an
inter-faith conference at Bangkok. I have twice visited
his monastery at Gethsemani in Kentucky; indeed I

said a requiem mass for him a few yards from where his body lies buried. In his last book, *Contemplative Prayer*, he distilled all his experience and study of prayer – he was working on the galley-proofs just before his death. As a monk he maintained his regular community worship and his reflection on the scriptures. Yet he saw that the heart of prayer was not in intellectual reflections, but in communing with God within. He wrote:

Prayer begins, not so much with 'considerations' as with a 'return to the heart', finding one's deepest centre, awakening the profound depths of our being in the presence of God, which is the source of our being and our life.

Another influential writer in this recent renewal of prayer was the French Benedictine, Père le Saux. He was deep in the Hindu–Christian dialogue on prayer, but never advocated, as others have, a shallow synthesis of Hindu and Christian spiritualities. With another French priest he founded an ashram which I have visited at Shantivanam in South India and he took the Indian name Abhishiktananda. Later he lived as a hermit in the Himalayas near the source of the Ganges. He died at Indore in 1973. In a small book, simply entitled *Prayer*, which has had a wide influence, he wrote:

Praying is simply believing that we are living in the mystery of God, that we are encompassed by that mystery, that we are really plunged into and immersed in it, like the air that surrounds us and penetrates the tiniest hollows of our lungs.

The immanence of God is, then, an essential element in our Christian spirituality; God is within us as well as above us. But there are real differences, it seems to me, between many forms of eastern meditation and Christian meditation or contemplation, partly because our concepts of God are different. Much oriental meditation aims at bringing us to a serenity within ourselves, which may clearly be a good thing. But Christian meditation aims above all at our letting the Holy Spirit build up between God, supremely disclosed in Jesus, and ourselves a deep relationship of love and trust; and serenity may come to us as a by-product. I elaborate a little further on this difference in my book, *Prayer and Contemplation*. I would also like to say that some of the simpler forms of oriental teaching about posture and rhythmical breathing may be to some of us a useful *preparation* for our own praying.

Our Western tradition of prayer
For a long time not enough has been said, I think, in conventional Christian teaching in the West, about the immanence of God. This has been a serious neglect for it has been an essential part of living Christian tradition. St Augustine taught that God is closer to us than we are to ourselves. Mother Julian of medieval Norwich, writing about her experience and understanding of prayer, said:

> Our good Lord showed himself to us in various
> ways both in heaven and earth. But the only place
> I saw him occupy was in man's soul.

St Teresa of Avila in the Counter-Reformation wrote, 'We are not forced to take wings to find him, but only to seek solitude and to look within ourselves.' These are all people who have really explored the world of prayer.

We need always to remember how inadequate all human language is, when we try to describe the experience of prayer – or to describe human relationships. In both of these parts of our lives even the simplest words do not always convey exactly the same meaning. Let us

47

take as an example the word 'with' in human situations. You sit with a stranger in a crowded commuter train. You sit with your doctor in his surgery. You sit with a friend at home by the fire on a winter's evening. According to its superficial meaning the word 'with' means that you were next to each of these three people. But according to its deeper meaning the same word 'with' is trying to describe three quite different experiences of closeness. Similarly when we say we are 'in' God, we are speaking of God's immanence, but God has different modes or ways of immanence, different kinds of closeness. If we over-simplify and try to make them all alike, we shall spoil and impoverish our use of the word 'in'; and we shall fail to grasp the richness and the variety of God's dwelling in us and we in him.

Again we must try to keep in balance, as well, the transcendence and the immanence of God. We can reflect on all this in the classical books on Christian prayer. These are in turn rooted in the scriptures. So let us now glance briefly at the New Testament.

In God we live
Paul speaking on the Acropolis to the Athenians declared, 'In God we live' and quoted in support of this the Stoic poet Aratus, though to the Stoics God was little more than a life-force. This truth is given a clearer focus in Paul's letter to the Ephesians, 'There is one God and Father of us all who is above all and through all and *in* all.' Here is explicit teaching about God within us; and Paul is writing not for theologians in their studies or monks and nuns in cloisters, but for quite ordinary Christians in the world. He means them to reflect on this and absorb it in their daily living and prayer. How are they – how too are we – to grasp and live on this truth that God is within us, and we in him? We will come back to this question in the next chapter.

In Christ

Even more stressed in the New Testament is Christ dwelling in the hearts of ordinary Christians. How frequently the words 'in Christ' occur in the New Testament; in St Paul's letters alone 164 times. It is true that living 'in Christ' sometimes means our living together in Christ's body, the church. But more often in Paul's letters it means Christ our Lord dwelling in us individually and we in him. It is so in John's gospel; 'Abide in me and I in you'. These words about Christ dwelling *in* us give a fresh depth of meaning to the word 'in', a fresh depth to our experience of the divine immanence.

A striking verse in the letter to the Galatians tells us how this dwelling of Christ in us can take place.

I have been crucified with Christ; it is no longer I who live, but Christ lives in me; and the life that I now live in the flesh I live by faith in the Son of God who loved me and gave himself up for me.

Dr Newton Flew in his book, *The Idea of Perfection in Christian Theology*, made a masterly survey of the development of Christian ideals and of the practice of prayer through the centuries. In his comment on this verse he wrote, 'Something *new* had come to pass in the history of religion.' No Buddha, no Mohammed, no Stoic, no prophet had ever spoken, as Paul speaks here. And Paul means these words to be true, not only for himself, but for all Christians, for you and for me. How are they *to be lived in practice*?

I would explain them along the lines of Jesus' own words, 'If any man will come after me, let him deny himself and take up his cross daily and follow me.' Let us see what these words involve for us.

First, to *deny* ourselves does not mean to undervalue ourselves or to have a 'low self-image'. On the contrary we must treasure ourselves, yet not put self and security in the centre of our lives, but rather Christ himself. We try to entrust the whole of ourselves to him. What we need is not self-depreciation, but a gradual revolution. This inner revolution is similar to that made by the medieval astronomer, Copernicus. Before his time we thought that the earth was the centre of everything and that the sun went round us for our convenience to keep us warm. Then Copernicus proved that the sun was the centre, at least of the solar system, and we on our earth are to go round the sun on our God-given path, our orbit. That is the kind of revolution we need.

Next, this denying self, this inner revolution, means taking up the *cross*, as Jesus said. The cross does not necessarily involve enduring pain or living an ascetical life, but getting rid step by step of our own self-centredness. The cross is a capital I with a small horizontal bar to cross it out.

Then this taking up the cross is not something done once for all, but something which needs to be re-done *daily*. In our modern times this taking up the cross may have for us a definite, decisive beginning. This was clearly so with the early Christians. They accepted the Christian good news that God himself had come to them in Christ, and they were baptized into Christ and his Church. They said that with Christ they died to their past, and then rose with Christ into newness of life and the joy of the Risen Lord. But they knew that this baptism was only the beginning, and that they must then continue to follow Christ, to die daily to self and to rise daily with Christ in his new life. So it should be with us as well.

This is our deeper understanding of the divine immanence. It is God in Christ living in us and we in him. This means living a full life, a disciplined, though not diminished, life, developing the hidden gifts God has given us, going on with our Copernican revolution, and so helping others also to find and to follow confidently their path, their orbit with us.

In the Spirit

There is a third way in which the New Testament
speaks of God within us – the dwelling in us of the *Holy
Spirit*. How often it speaks of our living in the Spirit! It
contrasts life in the Spirit with life in the 'flesh'. But
what do these phrases mean? Not what many modern
people think. Dr Newton Flew in his book puts it
clearly:

> To live 'in the flesh' means to live in a world
> where self is the centre. To live 'in the Spirit'
> means that the Spirit of God dwells within, we are
> aware of his presence, and by him can be led into
> newness of life.

So living in the Spirit is yet another way of speaking of
the inner Copernican revolution we all need; and that
revolution can happen in us because the Spirit is given
to us. We need to collaborate with him, but he begins
the change – sometimes before we are fully aware of it –
and he sustains us all the time. It doesn't happen all at
once; it is a long, gradual process, though it may well
have some decisive moments within it. It is true that we
have to continue to watch out for signs of self-centredness in our lives and then oppose them. But the Christian life is not an anxious struggle. It is welcoming this
gift of the Spirit into ourselves and living in his
strength. For deep in us is not only 'the river within' of
natural energy, but also the power and the leading of
the Spirit. 'The love of God has been poured into our
hearts through the Holy Spirit, who is given to us.'

This divine power within us should shape us as we
make our daily journey, as we mature into our true
selves. Then we can live our lives, not pushed about by
outside attractions and pressures, but quietly and confidently from within.

Trinity and Immanence

My young Oxford friend was mistaken – though understandably so – in thinking that we believe God is like a feudal monarch. I trust it is now being made clear in this book, specially in these last few paragraphs of this chapter, that there is within God himself what we can only call the flow of mutual love between Father, Son and Holy Spirit, *Amans, quod amatur, amor*, 'he who loves, what is loved and love', as St Augustine said.

More than this, there are ways in which we men and women can participate in this interchange of divine love. In the seventeenth chapter of John's gospel Christ prays the Father that '*The love you have for me may be in them*'. It means that the same love which unites the Father and the Son, may actually be in us.

Further, our receiving this divine love ourselves, our experiencing it and showing it to the world is *the way* in which we can help others to believe and to know God's great purpose of love. For Christ also prays to the Father for us all, 'that I may be in them and you in me, so they may be completely one, in order that *the world may know* that you sent me and that you love them as you love me'. Then they and we together can be used to carry out his purpose in the world of our times.

The door through which we can go and take our part in God's own purpose of love for the human race is prayer. So let us turn now to prayer that is real.

PART THREE

PRAYER
THAT IS REAL

6

Prayer that Never Stops

'The Practice of the Presence of God is the only part of
prayer that really matters.' What an over-statement it
sounds! But you and I may discover it to be true. How
often B. K. Cunningham used to say those words. He was
never narrowly 'religious', nor did he wish his students to
be. He spent twenty-five years between the wars in
Cambridge, preparing them for the ministry. He lived for
them. He had a sure eye for our very varied needs. He was
always affectionately called 'B. K.'.

Unceasing love and prayer
Paul says the same thing as 'B. K.'. What a contrast to
the conventional advice we hear nowadays – 'try to
pray morning and night, and don't forget to go to
church'! 'Pray without ceasing', Paul boldly says – and
to slaves and their bosses, to fathers and mothers
perhaps with families of ten in those days. How could
they – how can we – do it? Let us try to be realistic
about this and practical. Another part of our human experience may help us. Lovers and dear friends are not
only close to one another when they are talking to one
another. Even when they cannot meet and see one
another, love flows between them like an underground
river – and so they sustain one another. A young
American couple recently talked to me together about
this. He said, 'Even when I am in a hectic, high-
pressure sales conference, the thought of my wife and
her love helps me to keep my cool.' She said simply,
'Yes, even when we are apart, we're still really close to
one another.'

55

Prayer that never stops

It can become like this between God and ourselves. This is clear in a small book of another friend of mine. It has travelled thousands of miles by plane in my pocket. It is *The Practice of the Presence of God* by a seventeenth-century lay brother in Paris, Brother Lawrence. It is a collection of his personal conversations and letters. He tells us he realized the presence of God in his monastery kitchen, when several people were calling for different things at the same time, as much as when he was in chapel receiving the Lord in Holy Communion.

That experience sounds far beyond us. It was far beyond Brother Lawrence at first. He says so himself. In his early years in his community he was full of doubts and difficulties. He tells us how we too could grow into this continuous awareness of God. 'We should', he says, '*establish* ourselves in a sense of God's presence by *continually conversing with him*.' You and I too could do this in our busy days. It would make no extra demands on our precious time. But I find myself – and perhaps you do as well – talking not with the Lord, but with myself. How easily we find ourselves grumbling to ourselves; this makes us and others miserable; and it certainly doesn't solve our problems. Would it not be better to speak there and then with the Lord? He has told us that he is always with us – to halve our worries and to double our joys.

This *awareness* of God isn't only thinking about him, nor is it always having a warm feeling of his closeness; it is something deeper, and it grows like the love between that American couple.

But you may say, 'This awareness of God is all right for people with sheltered lives.' Yet remember Brother Lawrence had been a soldier in the ferocious Thirty Years' War. He was wounded and limped for the rest of his life. Then he had been ordered about as a nobleman's servant. Even in his community he had to travel about to buy provisions. Yet with all the stresses of his life, he grew into this constant awareness of God. What he has to say is still so vital to us. I want to find a new way to show what it could mean for us – and what it does not mean.

Praying-without-ceasing in today's world
None of us can ever stop thinking and feeling all day long. Even when we are dreaming or sleeping or are unconscious, some kind of feeling and thinking is still going on. And, whenever our eyes are open, none of us can stop seeing.

All this continuous thinking, feeling and seeing is always going on in God's presence. God, because he is God, is omnipresent. For Paul, as we have seen, said in Athens, '*In* God we live'; and he wrote to the Ephesians that God is not only above all, but is also '*in* all'.

How then can we in a practical way come to be aware of this fact – the fact that all this continuous feeling, thinking, seeing is actually taking place *in* God? It really is so, whether we happen to be conscious of him or not.

We ought not to try to be aware of this by thinking about God consciously all the time. This would be bad for our mental health. It would also mean that we should not be doing our best in many of our exacting tasks. When, for example, you have to feed a mass of complicated data into a computer, God means you to give your total concentration to that task, and not to be half-thinking about him.

This is amusingly illustrated in a story which David Sheppard, the Bishop of Liverpool, tells against himself. He was playing cricket in a test match. He had been recently ordained priest. In the outfield he dropped a catch. An Australian spectator shouted at him, 'Hey, parson; keep your eye on the ball and take your mind off God.'

57

In contrast, let us now think of occasions when we can be thoroughly entering into what we are doing – and yet at the same time aware of God himself in the situation. While out hiking, our eyes rest on the beauty of the countryside or the grandeur of the mountains; our ears pick up the murmuring of a stream; we feel that our muscles are swinging into a good rhythm – and at the same moment there is in our hearts a song of joy and of praise. We do not superimpose this praise of God on to the exhilaration of our hiking; we experience the praise as part of our total activity.

When we go to a party, we should really enjoy the total experience of the party; and in our human enjoyment we should simultaneously share our joy with God who is there, himself the source of the vitality and charm of our fellow-guests. Mary must in this way have enjoyed and praised God for the new wine as part of the total pleasure and joy of the wedding at Cana in Galilee.

Perhaps we meet a young graduate giving a year of his life to work in some rather inadequate anti-drug clinic. As he shares with us his achievements and problems, our silent thanking God and interceding should be as much part of listening and encouraging as is our breathing.

When we visit some shut-in older person, struggling against the pain and frustrations of a crippling arthritis, let us train ourselves to listen, to give some practical help and to pray simultaneously.

Our silent praying then becomes not an additional duty, but an integral part of entering into the whole situation. 'He prayeth best who loveth best.' At all such times we don't, as people sometimes say, bring the thought of God into the situation; rather we are aware that already he is in it.

This is important in our caring for all whom we meet; and it is important also for our maturing into our true selves. For we all must have noticed in ourselves the way in which we normally reflect on all our feeling, thinking, seeing. We think almost automatically about how it is all going to affect us individually, personally. So our reflecting becomes a private monologue. What we need of course is to discover how all this continuous feeling, thinking and seeing can be shared at once in dialogue with God, in whom we are always living. This change from monologue to dialogue will transform us from being self-centred to God-centred men and women. This is again the inner Copernican revolution we all so much need in order to become our true selves. And it will lead us to this joyful confidence in God on our own particular journey of life.

This unceasing prayer is clearly not confined to conscious words of prayer. This prayer that never stops happens *whenever* the mystery which is ourselves really meets with the supreme mystery of God.

If we are now seeing the practical importance of this prayer that never stops, let us not be vague about it. We need now to plan. And we must not be discouraged by lapses. We have to plan and re-plan, both for unconventional praying and also for special times for praying. Yet plans alone can't do it. Love can.

Unconventional praying

Let us think again of that young American couple. How had their mutual remembering of one another and their love grown so strong and so sustaining? And he often had to be away on long business trips. It had grown in two ways. First, they had little reminders, which made them think of one another at all sorts of moments – catching sight of a photograph, of a holiday souvenir and of the dear, familiar handwriting. Secondly, in spite of all the pressures, they also made and guarded special times together – though perhaps seldom as long as they would have liked.

It will be so with us, if we are going to pray-without-ceasing, to practise the Presence of God, which is in effect *sharing our life* with God, to us the beloved One.

So first of all it means making the habit of praying in all sorts of unexpected, unconventional ways. Ann and Barry Ulanov, two American academics, who have interested themselves in the psychology of prayer, write in their book, *Primary Speech* (SCM Press, 1985),

> Praying starts anytime, especially at unexpected times. We will find our own way to converse with God, drawn instead of pushed. What is wanted is not outward compliance with the rules, while inwardly we chafe in rebellion and grievance. No deals, no bargaining with God. No righteous puffing up over how splendidly we keep the rules. Our prayers tell us in every possible way that God wants a desiring heart, a glad heart, an angry heart, a fearful heart – our heart just as it is, freely given and freely exposed.

It is often those who pray in this spontaneous and quite unselfconscious way who can bring joy and strength to others. Temple Gairdner and his wife Mary returned to Britain for their first furlough from Cairo. He was exhausted from mastering Arabic and from trying to handle lively debates on Islamics. While in Scotland he received a letter from a friend at Exeter in a serious depression. He dashed down to stay with him. Afterwards this friend wrote:

> In those days, by music, walks and prayer, such as I had never known before, he lightened the whole cloud. His life and prayer seemed to be of the same pattern. It was not methodical, it was often ejaculatory, staccato, explosive, absolutely unorthodox, but it was genuine. To pray with Gairdner was to learn how a man who lived with God could talk very naturally with him.

This closeness, this infectious joy and healing were the overflow of Gairdner's way of praying.

And a mother told me about her spontaneous prayers. Their young children patter early into their parents' room. While getting herself up, she prays briefly amongst children's chatter in this sort of way: 'My God, you are real; you are the love we see in Jesus. Here we all are. Help us really to care for one another. We can't do it ourselves. Give us all your love.' A prayer which I am sure rejoices God our Father. And all through the business of the day let us keep on speaking with God. These have been called 'arrow-prayers'. I like the idea, but I dislike the name. It sounds as if we dart off prayers to a God who is far off. But in fact God is, as you remember Augustine said, nearer to us than we are to ourselves.

Planned times for praying
If we are going to become aware of God always, we need also special times of prayer. For married couples or close friends to experience the continual sustaining power of love, they need not only spontaneous loving thoughts of one another, but they also need their carefully planned and guarded hours together. We know how vital these are.

Human experience makes this clear. I refer now to sad experiences. There are around us many unhappy marriages, separations and divorces. There are plenty of reasons for all this. I myself wish to judge no one. But you will agree that one of the reasons for these sad experiences is that the partners let themselves get too busy. I know how easily it can happen. They haven't enough time for one another. Even when they have time, they are often so tired or restless that they only talk about superficial things or slump in front of the TV. They do not share their inner fears or joys. They do not listen to one another in depth.

Equally we need somehow to make time to be quiet with God. These two desires, for time together and for time alone with God, are not selfish desires. For it is these times which help to begin to enrich with love all our relationships, even those strained relationships which we all know in our workaday world.

'Intimacy', the Benedictine monk, Sebastian Moore, has written – and what he has written applies both to our human closeness and to our closeness to God – 'Intimacy should not be regarded as an insulation from a heartless world, but on the contrary as a wholesome contagion in a heartless world.'

7

Praying with Eyes open to the World

One of the joys of my life is the many friends I have, all sorts of men and women. We often talk about ourselves and our praying. What they say about their own prayer is sometimes so moving, so honest and so infinitely varied. I am now convinced I must never say to anyone, 'This is *the* way to pray.'

One of these dear friends was Max Warren, the general secretary of an Anglican missionary society, a wise counsellor, always reading, always writing. When he was seventy-three, he thanked me for my book, *Prayer and Contemplation*, and sent me a handwritten letter of seven quarto sheets about his own prayers. He said too modestly that he was 'no good at prayer'. During his life only three books about prayer, he said, had helped him: the first he used as an undergraduate, the second was given him by Mary, his wife, when they were engaged, and the third he kindly said was my own. He admitted that he could never 'be still and know God', because his mind was always 'racing'.

But all through the day he prayed almost continuously with eyes open to the world. He wrote to people in half the countries of the world. Hour by hour he offered up to God his tasks, one after another, as living prayers for them. He wrote:

> Intercession for me is so much part of my life that I cannot really define or describe it. It is first and foremost the offering of love, something I do for others, not least because I know how much I owe to them.

63

He was deeply a man of prayer, that prayer by which
the whole earth is 'bound by gold chains about the feet
of God'.

Max knew that this kind of constant praying could be
little more than 'wishing people well'; unless it was
linked with a constant awareness of God and his love,
with what we have called 'the prayer that never stops'.
On that Max Warren and B. K. Cunningham, who
were at Cambridge at the same time, would have
agreed.

Growing in awareness of God.
This is so fundamental. Then why is it that so many
people do not grow in this awareness of God – even
many who say their prayers and go to church regularly?
Certainly it is partly a question of our temperaments.
Yet do we not too easily make temperament an excuse?
We forget that the Spirit is within us in order to trans-
form us. Should we not expect, as St Paul says, to be
changed into the likeness of the Lord through the
Spirit?

Do we really desire this constant awareness of God
and his love? We cannot achieve it for ourselves. It is a
gift from God. 'My presence shall go with you.' He will
give it us if we come with *open* hands. How often, how
sincerely do we pray for it? It is rather like human love.
We experience love as a gift, beyond our deserving.
Yet we need to show ourselves open to it. René
Voillaume, a well-known spiritual guide, has said, 'The
test of whether we really love is that we long to love
more.' It is the same with the desire for awareness of
God's love.

Looking with open eyes
One practical way of growing into this awareness of
God is to make the habit of looking at those we meet
with open eyes, and with prayer for them in our hearts.
Aren't some of us perhaps more like the priest in Jesus'

parable, 'who walked by on the other side' and didn't notice the man who had been mugged on the road to Jericho? And the busier we are, the more easily we become like that priest.

Similarly when we read a book, we should read it with sharp eyes to find out the truth; and at the same time we should be praying that we may share the truth with others. In the same way as we read newspapers, listen to the radio or watch the TV, we should learn to evaluate, and at the same time to intercede. You may ask what practical difference will this make to us – I would answer with Ann and Barry Ulanov, 'Prayers are answered by our being drawn more thoroughly into the life of God.' Who can tell what ultimate influence that may have for ourselves and for others?

Our intercessions should, I think, be concerned primarily with – but not only with – those who are actually round about us. I believe we should do much of our praying immediately on the spot in our hearts. This is what Madeleine Delbrêl called *la prière à vif*. We should not say, 'I will remember to pray for So-and-so tonight'. No, let us pray here and now. This, as we have just seen, would help to remove that cool casualness with which we sometimes treat one another; it would gradually lighten and transform our whole life together, as the leaven in the parable changes the dough into bread.

A pattern for special times of praying
A husband and wife, happily married, think of one another frequently during the day, but they also look forward to sitting down and talking over the day together. So we should speak to God often during the day, but we also need to make time to, as it were, sit down with God and go over the day with him.

Many people pray last thing at night. They should do so, if that is the only time they can manage. But a friend of mine, who is a schoolteacher, drives to her cottage in

65

another village, makes a cup of tea and then prays; for her, prayer comes first, before marking notebooks, cleaning the house or keeping an attractive garden. I myself find twenty minutes about that time suits me well, and I look forward to it, like meeting with a friend. I don't mean it always feels very moving. Nor is conversation with a friend always 'something special', but we go on with it because this is how friendship is built up.

Prayer times are often difficult for students and academics to find. I was teaching at Bangalore; and I suggested to a group of faculty and students that late afternoon or early evening was a useful time for prayer. A faculty member said that was quite impossible for him and that he had so heavy a workload that he had to work through until after midnight, and then he was too tired for prayer. 'Why not pray just after your meal,' I replied, 'before your evening's work instead of after it?' He said to me appreciatively a week later, 'Thank you, Father, for your suggestion; I've prayed better – and I have worked better.'

For some other people it is even more difficult to arrange these times for prayer, especially mothers with several small children or doctors in training in hospitals. We must not worry if sometimes we just cannot find these times. What matters most is not these particular times, but our desire to live close to God, to share all our lives with him and to keep praying with eyes open to the world.

How best to use our special times for prayer
Then what shall we do with our particular times of prayer? The most important thing is to be really honest with God. See that it is the *actual* you who is praying to God. Say how you feel, as the psalmists and Jeremiah did in their prayers. Unconventional language is not irreverent language. True, God is above us, but he himself tells us through Jesus that he wishes us to speak

with him informally as to a dear father or a close friend.
I like actually to say my words of prayer quietly to God,
and not just to think my prayers. For if I do this, I find
my thoughts wander less and it helps me to grasp the
reality of God's presence with me.

I sometimes find – perhaps you do too – I need to
quieten down before prayer. Music can help; I have a
favourite Bach flute sonata or a cassette of young
people singing at Taizé *Ubi caritas et amor, Deus ibi est*
– 'Where charity and love are, there is God'. So can
poetry or a page or two of letters about prayer; my
favourite letters are those of Francis de Sales, Bishop of
Savoy in the seventeenth century, each so clear, so personal. Yet we have to watch ourselves or this may
become a diversion from prayer rather than a 'lead-in'
to prayer.

As you may have guessed, I like to pray spontaneously. Yet even so I like to have pattern for my praying,
but not a rule or a strait-jacket. Love doesn't live in
strait-jackets. The purpose of my pattern is to remind
me that prayer is not ask, ask, ask. Prayer is letting a
balanced friendship grow up between God and ourselves through the Spirit.

Adoration
Let us when we begin to pray say nothing. Let us
realize first what an extraordinary thing is actually
going to happen. We can't imagine how it can be. But
we are sure of it, because Jesus has told us, and he is
the one who really knows God and his deep care for us.
We ourselves don't begin our praying, he tells us; God
does by the attractive power of his love. We let ourselves respond to his love, although I agree it doesn't
always feel like it. 'His father saw him and had compassion, and ran and embraced him.' This is what God
with his ever-present love does for us; I need – and you
need – this truth; let us ask the Spirit to make it sink
silently deep within us.

67

So our praying should start not with the problems of the world or our needs, I think, but with adoring and praising God. We can adore him in silence or in our spontaneous words or in traditional poetic phrases: 'Let all that is within me praise his holy name.' Whenever we use such set phrases, let us put ourselves right inside them, so that they express our love.

God doesn't want our praises as flattery, but because he in his love knows that praise is so good for us. Praise disinfects us from egoism – first in our praying and then progressively in all the service of our lives.

Reconciliation

The more we realize in this way the light of God's love, the darker our failures and our un-love will look. This is not the moment for lengthy self-examination. If you should remember faults, tell God at once you are sorry. Friends and partners are wise to apologize and forgive one another at once. We don't want small faults to build up into a wedge either between us and those we love or between us and God.

Whenever you confess, don't hurry on to some other prayer, but rather stay in silence and realize the wonder of your reconciliation. Personally I then slowly make the sign of the cross. In prayer as in friendship and love some of us need outward signs. This sign of the cross reminds me clearly that the Lord came down from heaven, stretched out his arms on the cross and rose again to bring me back to God, forgiven and reconciled.

Thanksgiving

After this moment of reconciliation we should naturally wish to say 'Thank you' – for forgiveness and for so many other things also. Let our words of gratitude pour out. Words of thankfulness and appreciation keep our friendships and family relationships alive and warm. And so it is also with our love for God.

As Paul tells us, let us be thankful under all circumstances; and we can with a threefold thankfulness. First, we should express our gratitude for natural blessings – food, sleep, health, music, flowers, those we love and those who love us, and for the deep, mysterious 'river within us'. Let us not take these everyday things for granted. Our prayer and friendship with God should be rooted in the happenings of ordinary life. The real God is the God of the ordinary.

Secondly, we should thank God for supernatural blessings, especially for God's own love brought to us in Jesus, and then for the scriptures and the eucharist, the prayers of our friends and dozens of other ways his love comes to us. The supernatural is always with us like the air we breathe.

Thirdly, we should try to thank God for some of the hard things of life. But we should not hesitate first to complain to God. We must be honest; we must not pretend we are more 'spiritual' or more 'resigned' than we are. Then afterwards let us try sincerely to thank God. For, as we have seen, these hard things can help us to become more mature and more understanding and loving to other people in their troubles.

Thanksgiving helps us to deepen our confidence in God. It strengthens us to leap out of the bonds of the past into God's future for us. So we can journey more confidently in our service of the men and women of today and tomorrow. This leads us to our responsibility of praying for them.

Intercession
Always let us be sure that we are really speaking to God himself. Let us share with him frankly the desires of our hearts.

What we can do in our prayers – and what a responsibility and joy this is! – is to bring others to the Lord. It is what those men in the gospel did when they carried on a stretcher their paralysed friend to him. We bring them, as it were, into a situation where God's mighty love can be focused on them. With a magnifying glass we can focus the sun's rays on a piece of paper and set it alight. The sun supplies all the heat, but it is ineffective without the lens. Whenever we intercede, we need only look confidently to the God of love and hold steadily the lens of prayer. 'Without God, we can't; and without us, God won't' said St Augustine. God in his wisdom and love normally *waits* for us to collaborate with him. His purpose is, I suppose, to train us to realize our dependence not only on him but on one another through our mutual loving and praying.

I am often asked how we should pray for others in our own prayers. I myself find it hard to pray for groups of people vaguely. Jesus prayed, 'Simon, I have prayed for you that your faith fail not.' I know intuitively I must pray for people by name. If I know them well, I usually just open my heart to God about them. The more open I am with God, the nearer I am to him, and so the more he can use me, my prayers and my actions to help others. Sometimes I rest in God's presence and pray for a particular person very slowly the words of the Lord's prayer or some other well-loved prayer, which expresses all our basic needs. At other times I feel sure I can best intercede in silence. My intercessions are, you see, not my words but myself. God listens, as Augustine says again, not to our lips but to our hearts. So I remain silent in his presence with those I am praying for in my heart and put myself into his hands for him to use me as he knows best. Indeed Neville Ward in his book, *The Use of Praying* (Epworth Press, 1967), has put it fairly and rather bluntly: 'The prayer that is mere request, without self-offering, is not prayer "in Christ's name" and it is not worth the time it takes to say.' How can we pray for anyone and not, if we have the chance, do something practical for them? Doesn't this test the sincerity of our praying?

Prayer, like charity, should 'begin at home', but not finish there. So I make a start by praying each day for those dear to me and those for whom I have special responsibility. Then I find my intercessions can spread out like ripples on a pond to the ends of the world. But how can we remember all those we should pray for? 'The palest ink is stronger', says a Chinese proverb, 'than the best memory.' So in a pocket-book I spread their names over the different days of the week. I revise these lists of names. Personally I keep them reasonably short. Then they remain an *aid*, not an obstacle, to genuine praying.

Let us *go on* asking what we in our hearts think would be best for them. God receives all our requests. Let us not be discouraged if God in his wisdom and love does not do what we ask. And notice what it was that Paul prayed for his friends at Philippi, 'This is my prayer that your love may grow more and more.' That is our fundamental need and particular needs are included in it. Perhaps our requests seem to be unanswered in order to help us to see what matters most. Love is what we all need so as to grow into our true selves. I hope I do not sound unfeeling to many who call to God in distress. I remember a husband returning before Christmas from abroad and writing to ask his wife what present she would like. She replied, 'Bring yourself; that's what I want most.' So we find it to be between God and ourselves.

Yet sometimes I and my friends need something more to keep us going on praying confidently for others. Here is something which has helped us. It is speculative, but I think reasonable. We know there are those profound depths within ourselves, where we actually overlap and touch one another below the level of consciousness. We experience them through intuition, through wordless understanding between close friends and in other ways. And this inner contact can extend far beyond our friends. John Donne wrote:

No man is an island, entire of itself;
Every man is a piece of a continent, a part of the
    main.

When I have admired the beauty of the isolated islands of
the Caribbean, I have remembered they are connected by
the sea-bed. And God has connected us with one another
in this way; and he intends this connection to be the
worldwide circuit of his love – love we all need.

Unfortunately instead of being transmitters of the
current of God's love, we are often – through our ex-
cessive egoism – insulators. But, as we intercede and
give ourselves to God, his Spirit transforms us into con-
ductors, like turning black insulating mica into pure
transmitting copper. This takes time. How it actually
happens we will see in later chapters. It requires not
only human love but also divine love. So Paul told his
friends at Philippi that he deeply prayed for them, not
only because they were 'always in his heart', but also
because his 'deep feeling for them all comes from the
heart of Christ Jesus himself'.

Prayer for oneself
'I have so many others to pray for', people often tell
me, 'that I haven't time to pray for myself.' I understand, for as you may well imagine, I have in my life
many to pray for. Yet not to pray for ourselves is a mistake on at least three grounds.

First, because of our work. It says in St John's
gospel, 'Abide in me and I in you' and 'Separated from
me you can do nothing'. It takes a long time even for
committed Christians to accept those words, to grasp
our profound dependence on the Lord. But, until we
do, we can't do our best for others. Without this sense
of dependence on God we become, as we have seen,
either bossy or too diffident. So day by day we need to
talk with God about ourselves and our work and then
entrust our lives into his hands.

Secondly, for the sake of our own maturity. To grow into our true selves on our journey of life, we have to talk about ourselves with our friends in order to build up the warm human relationships we need. We also need similar closeness with God. To cultivate that we have to talk with God too about ourselves. Without this friendship with God we can't become truly human. 'Man without God', Nicolas Berdyaev said, 'is no longer man.'

Thirdly, for the planning of our days. Praying about ourselves for a few minutes in the evening means to look 'from a distance' at how we have been getting on in the past day, and to plan a little for the coming day. We need to do this not anxiously or in too detailed a way. We can look at it again the next morning. We should also remain sensitive to what has been called the 'in-speaking of God', quiet indications in the depths of our hearts.

Trust

I conclude my prayers by asking God to deepen my confidence in him, which really is sharing in our Lord's own trust in the Father. We cannot manufacture it ourselves. Confidence, like love, is a gift. Like love, it grows through being expressed and exercised. The pressures of our world and the anxieties in our own lives sometimes seem to disorientate us – even during our prayers. So we have a constant need to ask God by his Spirit to deepen our confidence; and we need also to express the faith we have, either in our spontaneous words or perhaps in some lines of the scriptures.

I will love you, O Lord, with my strength;
The Lord is my rock and my defence.

Prayer, like the conversation of those who love each other, should be fundamentally joyful. The Latin-American poet, Ernesto Cardenal, a disciple of Thomas

Merton, now a cabinet minister in Nicaragua, has written, 'Joy can be a perfect prayer, because it is an act of confidence in God; and joy can sometimes be heroic.'

Let me say again. We must each discover what is the best way for us to pray. We are – and God intends us to be – all different. I've told you how I usually pray. It must sound more elaborate than it is. It can be half an hour or as short as five minutes.

You may have noticed that the initial letters of these six parts of my pattern – adoration, reconciliation, thanksgiving, intercession, self (prayer for myself) and trust – form a key word easy to remember, *artist*.

I am in favour of spontaneity in prayer and in friendship. But I have discovered that guidelines for normal occasions are useful. Many friends of mine like this same pattern, but we don't keep rigidly to it. I always treasure some words of Teresa of Avila, 'When I pray, I never know what I am going to say next, because it is love that speaks.'

8

Praying with a
Heart open to God

I have just finished one of the most intimately honest
books I have ever read. What an encouragement it is
for us ordinary seekers in our living, loving and praying. The author at the age of sixty-one writes:

> I usually look forward to whatever is left of my
> life with high hopes that I shall at last become in-
> creasingly aware of the presence of holy mysteries
> which surround us all. Someone has said that
> mysteries are not problems to be solved but
> realities to be contemplated. I believe this con-
> templation is the most important element in
> prayer.

He not only reflected about prayer; he prayed. When
he was at home, he tells us he normally 'meditated for
an hour a day, usually between five and six in the
evening'.

He had lived no sheltered life; he was no orthodox
believer. He was Philip Toynbee, a well-known re-
viewer for the *Observer*. He published his diary from
1977 to 1979, and called it *Part of a Journey* (Collins,
1981). He died two years later. He wrote about his wife
and himself, his work and his hobbies, his pleasures and
his lapses, his anxieties about himself and the world and
his moments of vision.

He was the son of intellectual, high-minded
agnostics. He ran away from his school at Rugby,
calling himself a communist. Vaunting his red shirt and
red tie, he was coached for entrance to Oxford by

monks at Ampleforth. After university and war service he remained, he tells us, 'in a fluctuating attitude of hostile fascination towards all forms of religious belief'. Then at fifty-one he experienced a conversion, which 'was so unsensational, so undramatic' that he doubted whether he had a right to use the word at all. By telling Sally, his wife, he registered himself 'as a believer of sorts'. He had a nervous breakdown. He persuaded his doctor to let him have electric shock treatment. The darkness lifted, though shreds and patches of cloud came back from time to time. Three months after this treatment he began to toy with the idea of writing his book.

Receptivity in prayer

I have told you this to make it clear that 'praying with a heart open to God', or meditation or contemplation or whatever you would like to call it is not for 'special' people, but for ordinary Christians and for ordinary seekers like ourselves.

Fundamentally praying is nothing less than sharing – or wanting to share – the *whole* of our lives with God. For this we need the prayer that never stops, growing into a constant awareness of God and his love – or as Paul says, praying-without-ceasing. 'But you can't pray all the time', Jock Dalrymple, a Catholic parish-priest, formerly a students' chaplain, says, 'unless you pray at special times.' For myself I have found I need two times of personal praying each day, besides going to church. I need an evening time for the kind of prayer I outlined in the previous chapter; but also an earlier time, for just 'being with God' with an open heart. Without both of these I have discovered the quality of my life as a priest and of my writing goes down hill. Some people may be able to combine the two. I and many of my friends need both. I have noticed that students, however busy they are, who go in for transcendental meditation, are required to set aside two periods a day of twenty minutes each.

In human friendship we need two things – distinct though not sharply divided – first, to give generously of our time and of ourselves; and also to be glad to receive, to be in an adult way dependent on one another. Some people haven't discovered the real depths of friendship because they have never learned this glad dependence. Self-reliance can, it is true, be useful. But we may have been trained to be more self-reliant even than Jesus was. You will remember how in the garden of Gethsemane he said to his disciples, 'Stay with me, pray for me, I need you.' To become our mature selves we need to receive as well as to give in friendship – and also in prayer.

Finding time for quiet prayer
Jesus realized, I think, that he would not have in himself enough strength and love for all those who would crowd round him in his busy days. So he rose early and found a quiet place to receive from the Father all he needed for the coming day. We should see our quiet time in this light. Dietrich Bonhoeffer told his students in Nazi Germany, 'Meet Him first in the day before you meet anyone else.'

If first thing in the morning is impossible, let us try to fix an alternative time. For some immediately after breakfast is suitable. I found as a student I could use my first quarter of an hour in my room or in a library for prayer – with a New Testament on my desk along with my textbooks. Madeleine Delbrêl used to have her quiet prayer while travelling on the morning metro. I could not have done that. But she used to say the only noise which could there distract us from prayer was not the rattling of the carriage nor the talk of the passengers but the self-centred rumblings and grumblings in our own hearts.

Material for receptive prayer
All sorts of experiences can lead us into this quiet

77

prayer, by no means the Bible only. Never shall I forget an experience I had in Switzerland. I had been conducting some retreats. Then I was given a few days in the mountains of the Upper Engadine. We clambered up in snow to a high *col*; and there suddenly before us was an immense circle of 15,000-foot peaks, gleaming in the sunshine – the Morteratsch, the Bernina, the Roseg and all the rest. We stood in silence. Next I knew that I was accepting this wonder of God's creation into my heart. Then I felt inside myself that I was responding to this wonder, as you respond when you realize someone loves you. Finally I was sure that there was within me some action of God, something had happened inside. For as we came down to the snow line on the other side, I noticed those wonderful Alpine flowers low on the ground, the white crocuses, the blue ones and the violet soldanelles. I had seen them dozens of times before. But never until that day had I known such vivid colours. New eyes had been given me. And when at last we came to Pontresina in the opposite valley, the people looked different. They were no longer a vague group of Swiss villagers. Each face that evening had for me an individuality of its own. I had new sensitivity. How often since then in my early morning quiet prayers have I re-lived that day and re-experienced those moments and known again, I feel sure, the action of God within me.

It is this new sensitivity that you and I so much need day by day if we are really going to love and help other people on our journey of life. But we can't go off to the Engadine each morning. Yet I know pictures in the homes of my friends which can set me off in the same way; indeed I carry – between the pages of my Bible and in my wallet – photographs which often do the same thing. Philip Toynbee has told us how he trained himself frequently to look at, not just to see, a single tree, until it spoke to him. You may remember it was an almond tree about to break into blossom that awoke

78

Jeremiah as a young man to his call to serve God and his people as a prophet.

But for most Christians it is the scriptures that bring God and his love to us in this receptive prayer. So I would like to speak briefly of what the scriptures mean to me. There is something very special about them. For me they are like the Lord himself. He is in some indescribable way both divine and human; and so for me are the scriptures. The Bible is clearly an immense library, written by men; yet in various ways divinely inspired. This is why I feel I must use the scriptures in two ways, though not sharply divided from one another. The first way I call Bible-study or Bible-reading, in which we look primarily, but not exclusively, at the human side of the Bible. Who wrote these books? How were the events recorded? How was their deep significance drawn out? I have spent a good part of my life lecturing to theological students along these lines. I think it very important and we will glance at it briefly later in this book.

But now I will speak of the second way, which I would like to call 'Bible-praying'. In it we look rather at the divine aspect of the scriptures and try to find out how we can receive through them today the divine love.

Let me use another human analogy. If husband and wife or close friends have to be away from one another, how much they look forward to letters! When a letter arrives, they cannot open it fast enough. They want to know what has been happening, just as we read in the gospels and in the Acts what had been happening to Jesus or to Paul. But a letter of this kind gives us more than information; the handwriting brings also something of the personality and the love of the writer. This is why we can read these letters again and again. So we read the gospels and always find them fresh, for they are, as St Augustine called them, 'letters from God about his love'.

Methods of receptive prayer

There are hundreds of ways of 'Bible-praying'. Each of us needs to discover, perhaps with the help of a spiritual guide, the way best suited to us. In all of them, as distinguished from Bible-reading and study, we are concerned not chiefly with learning more facts, nor even primarily seeing what we ought to do, but above all with being met by God and so receiving his love for our daily lives.

In most of our lives, 'Bible-praying' starts with prayerful pondering of the scriptures, with slow reading well mixed up with praying. Next, as time goes on, some people want a more systematic method. It is often called meditation; it usually consists of reading the passage, of reflecting on it, of responding and then of seeing briefly how it all overflows into daily life. In this meditation it is the quiet responding to the Lord who comes to us which matters most; for that response is like a flame of love springing up in our hearts. This kind of meditation is like making a bonfire. The preliminary reading and reflecting is like collecting the wood, drying it, arranging it and then putting a match to it. But it is the leaping up of the flame – though perhaps not a very spectacular flame – which really matters.

As the years go by for many people, but not for all, meditation simplifies into the beginning of contemplative praying. After usually some years of meditation, the flame of love never or seldom goes out in our hearts. So we do not any longer have to collect many passages of scripture or reflections like pieces of wood. We need only by the help of the Spirit to blow on the glowing embers in our hearts and a flame of love silently leaps up. St Francis de Sales wrote, 'We meditate in order to love; we contemplate because we love.' We should not think that those who move gradually towards contemplative praying are better than those who do not; they are not better, only different. I have known wonderful Christians who right into old age have found all that they need is slow, prayerful reading of the scriptures. There is a little more detail about this normal development of 'Bible-praying' in my book, *Prayer and Contemplation*.

We have to discover for ourselves what parts of the scriptures help us most. For my 'Bible-praying', in contrast to my Bible-study, I turn nearly always to the gospels, just the words of the gospels by themselves. We want our friends' letters, not commentaries on them.

Perhaps it may help you if I tell you what I normally do with my early morning time of quiet prayer. This is not for you to imitate. But it may give you a few clues to discover your own way. I don't turn the pages of the Bible to find a suitable passage. Time in the morning is too valuable for that. I've done that the night before and have left the Bible open. As soon as I wake up, I try not to worry about the coming day. I look at an icon or a picture of the mountains. I tell God I trust him. I often say words of praise from psalms dear to me: 'O God, you are my God, early will I seek you', 'The Lord is my strength and my song', 'My heart dances for joy and in my song will I praise him'.

Then, as soon as I am ready, I settle down for my prayer. I usually sit in a firm chair, relaxed yet alert and open to God's love. William Hilton, a great man of prayer in the Middle Ages, said, 'I love to sit to pray, for then I feel more open to the Spirit.' I have no rigid plan. But usually I find myself following a fourfold sequence like my Engadine experience – *silence*, *accepting* God's love, *responding* to his love and *action*, something practical. Incidentally, if you like key words, as I do, you will notice that the initial letters of these four steps form the girl's name *Sara*.

First, I do nothing. For a few minutes I am still and *silent*, as amongst the mountains. It is so good not to feel hurried. I know God in his love is with me. We have the Lord's word for this. So I don't have to feel his presence. I only need to remember his presence. And he is there first. I just have to let myself be drawn to him by the magnetic power of his love.

Next, I *accept* God's love which usually comes to me through the passage I have read the night before. But I am not tied to it. So if some better passage occurs to me, I can follow that. Or sometimes through my window I see the sun rising or the fresh green leaves of spring or the autumn colours – any of these things can be a 'lead-in' for my receptive prayer. More often I keep to the verses I looked at the night before. I do not picture the Jesus of the past, because I am with the Jesus of today. *Every gospel passage brings me God's love in Christ, not a love in the past, but love now and for all the tomorrows.*

This is so, because Jesus at the start of his life work decided to love – and to do nothing else. Love was the motivation and the strength of all he did. Whenever Jesus taught, he looked into the eyes of his hearers, he read the needs of their hearts, and love gave him those words to say – that same love comes to me now. Whenever he healed, he by intuition saw their inner wounds and problems, and love did the healing – and again that love comes to me now. He went on loving the rich young man, even when he was not ready to leave all and follow Jesus. His love is challenging, yet not pressurizing, both then and now. Love gave Jesus the indignation and the courage to drive the traders out of the temple with a whip. His love gives us strength today.

It was his love again which led him to speak out with severe, hard words against the powerful Pharisees and lawyers. They had built around themselves a hard, protective shell of legalism, which isolated them from other people. Jesus couldn't help them and bring them forgiveness and God's love, unless he could first break through this legalistic shell. His severe words are inspired by love, then and now. The more Jesus loved in this strong, courageous way, the more his opponents plotted his death. Jesus saw death coming to meet him as he took his last journey to Jerusalem. Strengthened by love he courageously laid down his life to liberate us all. 'I have come, not to be served, but to serve, and to give my life a ransom for many.' Then he rose again to bring this new dynamic of love into our hearts right across the centuries.

Each morning God's eternal love is with me, not always felt, but always remembered and known, ever changing, but ever the same – like a well-loved view of mountains or of the sea. In the past I used to reflect on this love – Why could I be sure of it? How could it be more effective in my life? But now I do not so much reflect on it, but rather accept it.

Then, I *respond* to God's love. I have always tried to do this. Perhaps my prayer is now gradually becoming a little more contemplative. I know his love is with me. I try to bring it within me more and more. I respond in whatever way seems best at that moment. Sometimes it is in silence because this kind of prayer is, as we have said, like love, too deep for words.

Quite often it helps me to pray again and again peacefully a small phrase like 'Abba, Father', or 'My Lord and my God'. These words are not 'idle repetitions'. They are like the words which lovers say to one another to keep their affection flowing between them. So these little prayer phrases keep the flame of our love burning more steadily, like hands cupped around a candle flame to protect it from draughts; and then it burns more brightly. I often find nowadays this kind of praying fills a good deal of my morning time. Of course I am glad if some word or guidance comes to me from the Lord, but what I – and all of us – most need is his presence and his love. Often distracting thoughts come to us; let us not worry: these are not sins, only nuisances. Let us *keep on* turning to the Lord.

Finally, this interchange of love that is real then overflows into *action*. This is true, you would agree, of human love and of divine love. Yet friends do not meet 'to improve one another', but to enjoy being together. So we come to prayer not primarily 'to be improved', but to receive love and to grow in love. So it is only towards the very end of my time of prayer that I think of practical matters. Then I ask how this love between God and myself should help me to plan the coming day. I don't take too long over this or make too rigid a plan. There are small things that I decide on – a letter to be answered, a phone call to a lonely person, an apology to be made. I jot these down – and write a few words to take with me to encourage me during the day. It is these small things which gradually help us to grow into our true selves, made in the image of God, liberated by Christ, indwelt by his Spirit.

Naturally I pray for a few people dear to me or in special need, though my chief intercessions happen as I go through the day and at my evening prayers. I ask that my caring and praying may focus God's great love on them. Most of my personal praying is spontaneous. But I usually end my morning prayers with three set prayers. I pray first very slowly the Lord's prayer, desiring that God's rule may come into all the world. Next I add a favourite prayer of mine by St Richard of Chichester, asking that Jesus himself may be at the heart of my living:

O Lord Jesus Christ,
Most merciful Redeemer, friend and brother,
May I know you more clearly,
    love you more dearly,
  and follow you more nearly
    day by day.

Then I conclude with a prayer which a friend recently sent to me and which expresses how I would really like to live each day:

84

Lord God, grant that each one whom I meet today
    may be happier for it.
Let it be given me each hour today to know
    what I shall say;
and grant me the wisdom of a loving heart, so that
    I may say the right thing in the right way.
Help me to enter into the mind of every one who
    talks with me –
    and keep me alive to the feelings of others.
Give me a quick eye for little kindnesses
    that I may be ready in doing them,
    and gracious in receiving them,
    through Jesus Christ our Lord.

I hope I have not written in too much detail or too personally. I so much desire that you will find some sort of quiet prayer suitable to yourself.

'Praying', said Clement of Alexandria in the second century, 'is keeping company with God.' That is what we all want. We have to find our own way to do it – each day, if we possibly can. Real love is daily love; so is real prayer. Then we shall see how God can best use us truly to care for others in our modern world.

9

The Joy of Reconciliation

What happinesses there are in friendship and love. But sometimes a dark cloud comes down. The more you have loved, the blacker it is. It comes from some misunderstanding, some tension, some little bit of unloving. We can pretend that it doesn't matter much, and that we can somehow still manage to get along with one another. But the real closeness has gone; and it won't come back, until we try, in quiet, unambiguous words, really to explain ourselves and our feelings to one another. We sometimes shrink from this; it means giving up our pride and being honest; it is often so painful. But reconciliation can come – and then what joy!

Really loving God has led so many to fulfilment and joy. But on this road too there are dark and difficult times, we then need to face the truth about ourselves. Again we naturally shrink from such moments. We try to put them off and to settle for a kind of half-closeness with the Lord. But this doesn't really work.

Teresa of Avila is here such an encouragement for us. At first she was halfhearted and walked only the easy paths of the life of prayer; but eventually she tackled the steeper climbs and became so courageous and loving a woman. A modern Carmelite has written how Teresa did this:

She shared *everything with Christ*, both happy and unhappy events. And failure in virtue or other forms of unloving she would see as material to be laid on the altar, just as much as generous unselfish actions. The failure and the unloving need not be a stumbling block, if faced and accepted; they can be converted by trust and effort into *springboards* for personal change. Thus her approach was always positive; everything was fuel for the fire of the love of God.

Her mother died early, worn out with child bearing, when Teresa was only thirteen. She was a pleasure-loving youngster. Her strict father packed her off to a Catholic 'finishing school'. At twenty-one she entered reluctantly a large convent in Avila. She was half-hearted about prayer; she tells us she watched the slow hands of the clock, when she was supposed to be meditating.

Then after twenty years a change came, and she wrote, 'I could not possibly doubt the Lord was within me and I in him.' She learned to take a positive approach to all that came, the happy and unhappy events. She grew into her true self. She was loved by so many. She travelled about Spain founding small new convents, true houses of prayer and love. She prayed 'simply, intimately, securely' – and not without a sense of humour. She went on her journeys with a few nuns in a horse-drawn, closed-in wagon. Once after they had nearly been swept away crossing a flooded river, she said in her prayer to God, 'If you treat all your friends like this, Lord, no wonder you haven't many friends'.

Being reconciled and the kingdom of God
So let us try to see our being reconciled in its positive and full setting. Jesus came to reveal God and his love to us – and so to bring God's rule into our world. God's rule means gradually sharing our whole lives with him, being reconciled to him and also to one another. Jesus opened his life work with the words, 'The rule of God is at your doors'. Those who first heard his words could not have understood how much the message would

demand of him – and bring to us. But unless we understand this, we shall treat reconciliation either as a triviality or as a routine, as many have done.

To bring the rule of God into our world Jesus had to clear the ground for it, he had to overcome the force of evil. This evil could only be driven out by the power of love – the love which, as we have seen, was the motivation and strength of everything he did. All through his life work, day after day, he was undermining the power of evil by his love-inspired teaching and healing, by his love-inspired challenging and liberating. He went on and on courageously in his life of ever-present love until this love reached its climax on the cross. There, dying, he could say, 'It is finished'; his life task, his contest with evil was triumphantly completed. To make this victory clear to all, God raised him from the dead. It cost *all* this to bring to us the gift of forgiveness and reconciliation. Paul said that 'Christ died for our forgiveness and was raised to bring us reconciled to God'.

This costly action of God's love in Christ is a blessing and joy intended for the whole world. The apostle said, 'God was in Christ reconciling the world to himself'. But there can be no real reconciliation *en masse*. Reconciliation, if it is real, has to be accepted by us one by one. So Paul truly and unforgettably said, 'The Son of God loved *me* and gave himself up for me.'

Our living with open hands
We wonder at God's immense love. We are amazed at this forgiveness and liberation achieved for us at so great a cost. But are they really ours?

In ordinary life no one can give us an expensive present, if we keep our hands clasped and don't open them to receive it. So let us listen to what Jesus says about receiving, 'The time has come. The rule of God is at your doors. Repent and believe the gospel.' There are only two things for us to do to receive this gift from God. They should be as natural as opening our hands.

No tense effort. Only repent and believe in the gospel. The original Greek phrases make clearer what we need to do.

In this verse 'to believe' does not only mean to accept this statement of Jesus. It means to entrust yourself confidently to God, who comes to us personally in Jesus, as bride and bridegroom entrust themselves to one another. We may not be able to give ourselves at once to God in complete confidence. But the more we express our confidence in God through prayer, the more it will grow. So to receive God's gift we open one hand by our growing confidence in him; we open the other by a growing repentance, as the original Greek word, *metanoia*, is often translated. People used to be taught that repentance meant making a list of our faults.

Metanoia, our Copernican revolution
This word *metanoia* is something much deeper than that, and more exhilarating. It means literally a turning of the mind, a complete turnabout of our outlook on life, that Copernican revolution we all need. We can't do it by tense efforts ourselves. The Holy Spirit can make this transformation, changing us from within. Most of us at heart would really like this change to take place in us. We see that, if we became less self-centred, we should become more attentive and loving to others. We also know that this change would be the supreme way of showing our gratitude for all God's love to us.

Then why don't we let ourselves be changed by the Spirit of God's love? The reasons must be many and complex; but let us begin to examine what they are.

Looking at our lives
First, it is not to be miserable about our faults, but to discover our actual selves better, that we look at our lives. I have suggested we should do this in a brief check-over at our daily evening prayers. But from time

to time we do this in a longer, more leisurely way – in preparation for our Sunday Holy Communion, at the quarter days, at an annual retreat or a workshop on prayer. Lists of questions about sins used to be printed – perhaps they still are – to help people at such times not to be vague about their shortcomings. Unfortunately these lists can lead to a rather superficial – and perhaps legalistic – attitude to our failings. Deep down, our failings are failures in love. It would be more honest and more balanced not to concentrate only on our failings, but to look honestly at our whole selves and see how we now stand. This would include gratitude to God for what is sound and true in our lives; and it would involve recognizing how far we are responsible for our failings.

Secondly, I would suggest that we note both our specific failings, and also other telltale symptoms in our lives. We need to be clear about our failings – so as to be able to confess and acknowledge our responsibility for them and also to make a real and clearly-defined effort to cut them – with God's help – out of our lives. We, Christians, often aim so vaguely that we seldom hit the target.

Yet besides our failures we should note many rather strange things about ourselves which are not specific sins. Why, for instance, did a trivial item of news make us depressed out of all proportion? Why did some small forgetfulness of a colleague make us far too angry? What was the deeper reason why we forgot that appointment? The answers to this kind of question may tell us that something is out of order in us just below the level of consciousness. What is out of order there may be at least as significant as wrong actions we have done or right actions left undone.

Thirdly, when we wish to look at our lives, it might be better not to check ourselves by a list of rules or commandments, but rather to survey the various areas in our lives. How conscientious are we, for example, in the various parts of our job and of our home life? How well do we relate to the people we work with, and those we live with? How do we apportion our time? Do we ask the Spirit to show us what *not* to do? What about our efforts to pray-without-ceasing? What about particular times of worship and prayer, which nourish this constant awareness of God and his love?

Fourthly, we need to look more deeply and leisurely behind all the failings and defects. They themselves are like the spots on our faces; they point to deeper ills within us. 'At eventide we shall be examined about love' is how St John of the Cross put it. Our defects are fundamentally our failures of love, or even more our reluctance to let ourselves be transformed by love.

Forgiving and being forgiven
As we think of our own need of forgiveness, we cannot forget the words in the Lord's prayer, 'Forgive us our trespasses, as we forgive those who trespass against us'. God cannot pour his forgiveness into our hearts unless we open our hearts; and we open our hearts through our forgiving of others.

God asks us to be prepared to make reconciliation. Paul says, 'Live in peace with all men'; but then he adds, 'as far as it is your responsibility.' He means that we should make the first move, unless this would cause a needless and useless re-opening of old wounds. But if, when we have made the first step, the other person will not respond, we must not ourselves feel anxious or depressed. We must of course continue to pray. But we have done what we could. God does not ask more of us.

Reconciliation is so important, because it can have momentous consequences for others and for us. But how can we forgive in this way? It sometimes doesn't seem fair that we should have to forgive like this. But *all* of us have to, if we are going to live even moderately happy lives. I in my experience have known how hard it sometimes is to forgive. But it can be done. On a dark

91

December day Pope John Paul II walked into a prison cell in Rome and there in a quiet conversation forgave the man who had fired a bullet at his heart in St Peter's Square a few months earlier.

We need to admit first that we ourselves have been hurt and are angry; and probably we have, at least deep inside ourselves, hated this person. Only after we have begun to *separate* the wrong that was done from the person who did it, can we start really to forgive. And we often have to admit to ourselves that we may have done something to provoke the other by our own temper – or by our own coldness.

When we have made this separation, we are in a position to let the past go – without burying resentment down in our own hearts, which is always a dangerous thing to do. Then we have to *work at* forgiving the other. Most of us can't say, 'I forgive you', and then it's all over for ever. No, the hurt – and the hate – keep coming back. This is not surprising. Whenever we try to break some unfortunate habit, we know it is going to be hard work. We know we may even slip back into it. But we are resolved to come out of it; and in the end, with the help of God's love, we do. C. S. Lewis as a boy was hurt by a bully of a schoolmaster. For years he was worried by his failure really to forgive this man. It was only shortly before he died that Lewis was able to write to a friend, 'Only a few weeks ago, I suddenly realized that I had at last forgiven the schoolmaster who so darkened my childhood.'

God in his love is patient with us; and we have to be patient with ourselves in our attempts to forgive and to love others. Let us genuinely ask the Spirit to enable us to do this – and so break the spiral of anxiety and perhaps also of ill-health both for the one who did the wrong and the one who suffered it.

Confessing our faults
We look at our lives and our relationships with others,

not primarily to have peace in our hearts, nor even to get on better with others. We do it, fundamentally, to deepen our friendship with God for which we are made. As I examine my life, I do not think about it vaguely; I ask myself, 'Just where do I need forgiveness? What else ought I to say to God?' So as not to be vague, I write it down – in abbreviations. An absent-minded friend of mine, as he might leave it about, writes it in code! I set aside perhaps a leisurely half hour to do this. First, I am quiet. I am not coming, as it were, to knock at God's door. He rather comes to me to welcome me, exactly as I am. He longs for me, far more than I do for him. As I confess to him quietly and clearly, I know I am not wiping away my faults and turning over a new page in my life. It is God himself who is doing something very real inside me. He puts into me the forgiveness and liberation that Jesus brought into our world – through his unceasing love, his dying for us and his rising again. And, Jesus tells us, to welcome me brings joy to God himself.

Then I rest silent again, letting the divine forgiveness sink into my heart; and, as I said before, I like at this moment to make slowly the sign of the cross – a symbolic action, full of meaning for me, like a handshake or an embrace between close friends. It is only as I am assured of this forgiveness that I can enter into the real joy and freshness of life with Christ.

Absolution

Not one of us would wish that anyone else should intrude into this closeness between the Lord and ourselves. Yet nowadays many people need not only to receive this sense of forgiveness into their hearts; but they also need someone to assure them by a spoken word that they have received this complete forgiveness. This is very understandable; it is how our human nature normally works. God in his wisdom and love arranges that we shall receive so many of his gifts *through* others.

93

Our first experience of love, for example, normally comes to us through our mother's love. Our first knowledge of what life is all about usually comes through the lips of parents, teachers and companions. Similarly we can help one another to be assured of forgiveness and so be healthier and less anxious. We read about this in the letter of James. 'Confess your sins to one another, and pray for one another, that you may be healed.' Many of us must have experienced being helped in this way by friends. For obvious reasons we have to choose carefully whom we are going to confide in. The reformer, Calvin, said that a pastor should be, because of his calling and training, the most suitable person to give us this assurance.

Men and women have through the centuries needed this outward sign of forgiveness. The prostitute who cried at Jesus' feet in the house of Simon the Pharisee must have known in her heart that God would give her inner forgiveness as soon as ever she turned to him in repentance. But she knew she needed something more; she needed to hear human lips say to her, 'My daughter, your sins are forgiven; go in peace.' How many people received joy through Jesus' words in that way in his lifetime! Jesus knew that many would continue to have this need of outward assurance. So at Easter, while he was still with the apostles, he said to them, 'Receive the Holy Spirit. If you forgive people's sins, they are forgiven; if you do not forgive them, they are not forgiven.' Of course, no man can forgive sins, but only God. Jesus was saying to the disciples and to the pastors who would succeed them that they could in the future do for men and women what he had done in his days; that is, they could assure them individually that God himself had forgiven them.

There has been some reluctance to use this way of confession, perhaps because of its misuse in the past. All good things, like friendship and love, have also been misused; but that doesn't hinder us from using them well. I am glad that this way of receiving assured forgiveness is being more and more welcomed and valued. Not all need it, but many do.

I went as a student to my first confession, rather hesitant and nervous. I shall never forget the joy of absolution that day. Confession has gone on helping me down the years. I have watched it helping many others. I remember giving a week's course in Birmingham on the life of prayer. It was years ago about the time we finished with national military service in Britain after the war. A young man came to my course after a difficult time in the air force. Afterwards he said in a letter, 'I listened to what you said one evening about confession. A day or two later I knew in myself that this is what I ought to do. On the Saturday afternoon I was waiting in church with others for my turn to go into the little side chapel to make my first confession. I never felt so awful in my life. But no one will know what deep joy I felt when you spoke to me the words of God's absolution.'

Confessions are made like that in churches and also increasingly in less formal ways. People sometimes feel deeply moved, sometimes not. We just have to be honestly ourselves. The certainty of our forgiveness rests not on our feelings at the time, but on the Lord's own promise that our sins are in this way completely forgiven.

Inner healing

What I have already written is enough for many people. It will set them free to step out afresh on life's journey strengthened by God's love. But for some people more is needed. *Metanoia*, confession and forgiveness have been studied afresh in recent years – and not least in the Roman Catholic church.

Sometimes a person has examined his life carefully, confessed to God sincerely – and perhaps has also been absolved through a priest – and yet he has not come

95

through to an inner peace or shown much sign of vigorous life. An indication that something more is needed is shown, for example, when we still over-react with anger or fear to some trivial remark or incident, or when we are continually depressed without any obvious adequate cause. I do not refer to those small ups and downs of temper or minor depressions which come in almost all our lives. I mean those more powerful aggressive or negative feelings, which cannot reasonably be explained. They seem to be welling up from some past experience, which is just below the level of consciousness, or even much deeper down.

If these unpleasant feelings do not cause the person much trouble, we can perhaps help him to live with them and not to be too troubled by them, as sometimes it is not worth opening the scars of old, minor wounds. On the other hand, if these feelings are spoiling the person's life and causing distress to his family and neighbours, his doctor may recommend him to a good psychotherapist. This may cost much time and money. I have known men and women who have gone through long treatment, and in the end it has healed and enriched them and also enabled them to understand and – after suitable training – really to help others.

The troubled person may sometimes be able to help himself to find the hidden or half-hidden causes. He may remember times when he was hurt by sarcasm, when he was over-criticized, when he was terrified by some shock or when he felt rejected and unloved. Some of these hard experiences may be a long way back in childhood. But they have left a wound, still painful underneath, and still causing trouble inside. Yet we all know that Jesus himself, to whom the past is as the present, can walk through these hidden paths of our past and can heal today as he has always healed.

There are other troubled people who find it difficult to help themselves yet do not need highly professional treatment. But if they try to go it alone, they may get lost in the confused ways of their past. They really need to find a 'friend', or what Alexander Pope used to call 'a guide, philosopher and friend', to whom they can gradually open these past misfortunes. Many ministers and others too could be trained to help in this way. They need to be people of wisdom and sensitivity, of faith and of real prayer, and of course with no trace of unhealthy curiosity or pressurizing or subtle power-seeking.

Then this guide can walk with the suffering person in these hidden paths – and with Jesus himself – just as truly as Jesus walked with those disciples from Jerusalem to Emmaus on Easter afternoon. The troubled person could, when he is quite ready, tell Jesus and the friend just what was done, what was said and what it felt like – even if it costs some tears. He does not have to say who was to blame, but he should be ready to try to forgive. The friend will pray in silence and perhaps in a few spontaneous words. He is not there to judge, to apportion blame, but only to walk as a friend. He may, if asked, at the end lay hands on the troubled person or give any other desired help. But it is Jesus himself who is the real friend and healer. As in the days of the gospels, he always understands, appreciates and encourages. He listens; then, like the father who welcomed back his lost son, he embraces us and says, 'Come, cheer up, take my hand and my strength'. He himself does all the healing. Sometimes it comes more quickly than we expect; sometimes, as in all healing, it takes time.

Perhaps this is something for us to think about and to learn more about, specially if we know troubled friends of our own. I have met many people who have been helped in this way. I know a married couple who for years could not understand one another or talk deeply to one another; they are now lovers and friends. I know a priest who is now much freer, happier and more effective in his family and ministry, because the Lord helped him to re-discover and re-live a sad memory very early in his life, and so be healed.

This is not the way for everybody. But it is one of the ways alongside the main road of reconciliation, in which we can open our two hands in confidence and *metanoia* to receive from our ever-generous God the love we need for our life journey.

And then we can share with others what we ourselves have deeply received.

10

Praying Together and the Eucharist

At Nazareth I only had a weekend between teaching two courses in Jerusalem. They kindly put me up at an orphanage, overlooking the village. There was a chapel but no priest. So I asked whether I could celebrate Holy Communion for them on the Sunday morning. The sister-in-charge said, 'Wouldn't you rather have the Communion beside the Lake of Galilee?' That was soon settled. It was still dark when we left and drove down to the traditional site of Capernaum. For our altar we chose a large flat rock at the water's edge. With the waves lapping at our feet and the sun's first rays touching the hills on the other side of the lake, in that unforgettable moment, I celebrated the eucharist. *Jesus came – and comes – to us through this feast.* We know it because he promised it. Let us never lose our sense of wonder at his coming.

In the eucharist the Lord's coming stands out clearly in a wide perspective. For it is together we receive him. And we not only receive; in gratitude we offer ourselves to God with him in his perfect offering of love. Then, united as we are to him and to one another, God can use us to bring his kingdom into our world today.

Our need of praying together

I know a sceptical young woman, embittered by being deserted by her husband, who discovered God – and herself – through the joy and the caring of a small group of friends who really worshipped together. Often God's love comes in this way. How sad, then, that worship, which should be love received, responded to and overflowing, can put people off, as it did the young Philip Toynbee, by its sheer dullness.

Why is real prayer together so vital? It is because *God plans that his love should come to us through our fellowship with one another.* This was so for Jesus, as it is for us. Jesus received the divine love through his closeness to Mary's breast. It was there that the deep direct bond grew between himself and the Father. He continued to receive divine love, as we do, through human friends. He grew too in faith and confidence in God through praying together with his fellow-believers. So he worshipped with them in the village synagogue week by week. I don't suppose Jesus always found the worship exciting, for some of those old rabbis were, I guess, dull preachers.

What then can we do to make our worshipping more real? I would like to make four suggestions.

First, we should try, before our worship begins, to have time to remember vividly God's presence and love, as we do when we pray alone. A bishop, a friend of mine, who goes to many churches, said to me, 'Much worship is spoilt before it begins'.

Secondly, when we are asked to help in leading worship or are just joining in it, the important thing, if we are to avoid selfconsciousness, is to keep our eyes on God. Selfconsciousness blights worship, as roses are blighted by mildew.

Thirdly, our mutual love matters more than our numbers, although it is a joy to be with a great congregation praising God. When Jesus spoke about the effectiveness of two or three praying together 'in his name', he was not concerned about how many we are. He was concerned that we are really praying 'in his name'. That means that in our praying we are close to him and to one another. We then, as we saw in chapter 7, form together a great circuit of God's ever-flowing love. We transmit his love and bring blessings to others. This is why in our congregations and groups for prayer reconciliation and mutual love are so important.

Fourthly, we need suitable variety in our patterns of worship, for these can enrich one another. I myself have been equally grateful for the worship in a packed stadium at the vast World Council Assembly at Uppsala and at a small Quaker meeting at a Swanwick student conference; also for a monastic church crowded with Russian pilgrims at Zagorsk near Moscow, and a simple communion for a dying Swiss nun in her cell. I often thank God for these wonderful experiences, as in silence I prepare to celebrate the eucharist. I remember also how often I have received our Lord in the sacrament with a few students or a few close friends. These intimate memories help me to preserve that closeness and directness of my communion with him – which I also knew beside the Lake of Galilee – amidst all our joy together at the magnificent eucharists of the festivals.

The centrality and framework of the eucharist
How very much we owe to the ecumenical and liturgical movements, which have in these last fifty years brought new life to most of our churches. These movements reached a climax together in 1982 at Lima in Peru, when over a hundred theologians, Roman Catholic, Orthodox, Anglican, Protestant and Pentecostal agreed on a statement about the eucharist (and also about baptism and the ministry). This led to the 'Lima eucharist' being celebrated as the high point of the assembly of the World Council of Churches at Vancouver in 1983. The Lima document and liturgy remind us of what has been deep, though often obscured, in our Christian inheritance from the New Testament until today. They place Jesus' coming to us and indwelling us right at the heart of all our worship, living and serving in the world.

The eucharist is central, not because it happens to appeal to us, but because Jesus on the eve of his death and resurrection made it central. 'Do this in remembrance

101

of me.' Dom Gregory Dix, the Anglican liturgical scholar, wrote in a memorable phrase, 'Never has such a command been so obeyed'. The eucharist was celebrated frequently, at least every Sunday, in Christian congregations throughout the world until the Reformation. The reformers themselves, Luther, Calvin and Cranmer, wanted their people to receive Holy Communion each Sunday, but the reaction amongst their followers against medieval abuses was too strong for them to carry their point. But today these ecumenical and liturgical movements are restoring the eucharist to its central place in ever-widening circles.

The Lima documents underline this and they also show that the eucharist has a clear framework which many revised liturgies now follow. Further, within this framework they keep an appropriate place for some free, spontaneous prayer. This basic framework is given in the medieval classic, *The Imitation of Christ*: 'I need to be fed from two tables, the table of the holy word and the table of the holy sacrament.' The eucharist consists of two main – and balanced – parts, the feasting on the scriptures and the feasting on the sacramental gifts.

To share fully in the eucharist is rather like walking across hilly country. Climbing the first hill is our preparation; we confess our faults; God forgives and takes them away, so that they do not close our ears or dull our hearts as we go on to receive the gift of his love in the scriptures and then in the sacrament.

The top of the first hill is our enjoying and *feasting upon the word of God*, as we speak about a feast of poetry or of music. We read the scriptures here not for academic study, but to receive through them God's strength and love that we need for the coming days. There is next, as it were, a slight dip in our journey; and this is the place for the intercessions; these are now in more varied forms.

Now we come to the second hilltop of our eucharist, *the feasting on the holy bread and wine*. This itself has four stages, based on what Jesus did at the Last Supper.

First, the priest *takes* into his hands the bread and wine, as Jesus did at the Last Supper. This action is full of meaning for our everyday lives. The bread is a product of men's work. The wheat may have been grown in the prairies I know in Canada. Transported across the Atlantic, it has been made into bread by men and their machinery. This bread God is going to use to feed us with the strength and love of Christ. While we watch the priest take this bread, we could reflect on *how* we should be doing our daily work so that God may use our work too for the good of others.

Then the priest, again like Jesus, takes the cup of wine into his hands. How often have I watched in France and Switzerland and Germany the vines being cultivated, and the grapes grown and harvested. The sparkling wine, which nature and man have made, stands for our joy and togetherness in life. This wine is going to bring the divine love to us in this feast. So as we look at the chalice of wine, let us be thanking God for our fellowship together. How can we ever praise God enough for the joy that family, friends and love have brought to us? And *how* can our friendship and love better enrich other lives and bring them the divine love also – and specially those who have found difficulties in their personal relationships?

The second stage of this part of the eucharist is deep *thankfulness*. Like the Jewish father who presided at solemn meals and Jesus at the Last Supper, the priest, with the people, today, next express their gratitude to God – for the wonder of creation; for making us for friendship with himself; for Jesus our friend, brother and liberator through his being born at Bethlehem, his dying for love of us on the cross and his rising again at Easter; and we thank him too for the coming of the Holy Spirit to give us new joy and to make us his fellow-workers in the Body of Christ, bringing his reign of love into the world through all the ages.

We do all this in 'remembrance' of the Lord. This is an inadequate translation of the Greek word *anamnesis* in the scriptures. This word does not mean only our remembering an historical event, as we would the martyrdom of Peter and Paul. *Anamnesis* means God's bringing into the present moment Christ himself with all he has done for us and for all creation. As we eat and drink together we are actually being drawn into him and all his creative and liberating action. Indeed at the same time we have also a foretaste of God's final 'gathering of all things in one'. This we may find hard to grasp, but close friends also experience in anticipation a real part of the joy of their future meeting.

The bread and wine are in some wonderful way brought into this process of the *anamnesis* of Christ and his great actions; they become for us the sacramental sign of Christ's body and blood, which bring to us his strength and love. This mystery does not happen because we think about it or imagine that it could happen; it happens through the coming of the Holy Spirit in the eucharist and in ourselves, in ways quite beyond our understanding.

The third stage in this feasting on the eucharist is the solemn *breaking of the bread* at the end of the central thanksgiving prayer. St Paul says: 'The cup of blessing which we bless, is it not a sharing of the blood of Christ? The bread which we break, is it not a sharing of the body of Christ? We being many are one bread, one body, for we all partake of the one bread.' Receiving the holy bread and wine not only unites us to the Lord, but also to one another in him.

Fourthly, in this sacrament our Lord *gives* himself to us, as really and as personally as he came to Mary Magdalene at Easter dawn. The wonder of it all! He comes to dwell in us. We are also meeting one another *in* him.

Then after these two great hills in our eucharistic journey we descend again to the plain of daily life. As we come down, we make a short thanksgiving and offer ourselves afresh to God. We are sent back into the world with the words, 'Go in peace to love and serve the Lord'.

Before, during and after

I would like to write personally for a moment. As you may have guessed, my life is packed with travelling, lecturing, giving retreats and writing. But I treasure more than I can say the half hour of the eucharist each day. I was touched by some lines of Henri Nouwen, a priest who has taught spirituality at Yale and Harvard. He was writing to his father to comfort him after his wife's death.

> My whole being is rooted in the eucharist. I do so many other things and have so many secondary identities – teacher, speaker, and writer – that it is easy to consider the eucharist as the least important part of my life. But the opposite is true. The eucharist is the centre of my life and everything else receives its meaning from that centre.

This is true not only of many priests, but of other people too. It does not happen just through our sharing in the eucharist, even sharing in it frequently. Our eucharists need to be woven together. Then each one deepens our love of God and our confidence in him. Each time friends are going to meet, they look forward to it; they then enjoy being together; and afterwards they feel a continuing strength and closeness.

So *before* each eucharist we should think over what we need to bring to God for his forgiveness, what we particularly wish to thank him for, and what intercessions we would like to make. Then if we weave these thoughts of our own into the appropriate parts of the liturgy, we are making ourselves part of the eucharist.

During the eucharist itself, our sharing in it can be enriched by two kinds of closeness. We should first be close to our fellow-worshippers and sensitive to their feelings. We should be praying for them. If it is the custom of the church which we attend, we give them a greeting, with the words, 'The peace of the Lord be always with you' – our sharing with them not only our human friendship, but also God's gift of peace. But we have a second closeness not lessened by this human friendship, a closeness to God. Ruth Burrows, a modern Carmelite, writes of it: 'In the midst of our praising God together, we should be loving him and responding to his love, just as much as we do in our most precious and intimate personal prayer.'

After receiving the sacrament, personal prayer is so important – as we return from the altar, before we leave church and during the day – to deepen our awareness that Christ is really in us and we in him, so that we can bring him and his love wherever we go. Human fellowship at church is valuable; but it can sometimes crowd out deep, quiet gratitude to God. Gratitude, which is sincere, takes us a step further. For we pray in one of our finest Anglican prayers, the General Thanksgiving, that 'we may show forth God's praise, not only with our lips, but *in our lives* by giving up ourselves to his service'.

Prayer and eucharist, if sincere and real, lead us to put our everyday lives into God's hands for him to use to bring in his kingdom here and now.

IN THE REAL WORLD

11

Prayer and the Kingdom

'I say quite deliberately that the Christian religion, as organized in its Churches, has been and still is the principal enemy of moral progress in the world.' Bertrand Russell said this about Christians. Of course it is exaggerated. But enough of it is true to make it *stick*; and why?

His parents, both free-thinkers, died before he was four. He was brought up a lonely boy in the house of a puritanical grandmother. No wonder that he had his serious blind spots. He had lost all religious faith before he went up to Cambridge. He was always a brilliant thinker, a provocative character, and a man of courage.

Exactly what did Bertrand Russell mean by moral progress? The context of his words shows; it was steps towards the elimination of war, towards a fraternal society, towards racial equality. Christians have taken a leading part in working for these reforms, William Wilberforce, Lord Shaftesbury, William Temple, and Martin Luther King, to mention just a few. But we cannot deny that many Christians and Churches have done very little.

This is largely because of lopsided teaching about prayer.

Jesus, inaugurator of the Kingdom and man of prayer
Prayer means not narrow pietism, but involvement. Jesus did not preach prayer; he proclaimed the kingdom. The beginning of his message and its main plank, as we have seen, was 'The kingdom of God is at your doors'.

Yet Jesus was *par excellence* the man of prayer. It was through prayer that he was one-with-the-Father. It was this oneness with the Father, which gave him the love, the confidence, the strength he needed to be the herald of the kingdom and to bring it more and more into this world. For us too prayer is not just an individual *tête-à-tête* with God, to give us serenity on our journey and to bring us to eternity. Prayer involves us in the coming of God's kingdom into this world.

The phrase, kingdom of God, comes eighty-two times in the first three gospels. The word, which Jesus almost certainly used in Aramaic, his mother-tongue, was *malkuth*. It means the fact that God is ruling. It does not mean a particular territory with frontiers; nor can it stand for the universal Church with its baptized members within its boundaries; still less can it be a secular utopia.

On the contrary, the rule of God is *wherever God is liberating mankind from its evils* – ignorance, injustice, fear, poverty and disease. We might perhaps say the rule of God is wherever God is restoring and putting into action the original purpose which he had for his creation – including maturing us into our real selves, so that we can love and serve better in the world.

In Old Testament times the prophets looked forward to it and experienced it. But in an important sense *Jesus himself inaugurated the rule of God*, he gave it a new reality. Jesus spoke about it in his parables. The rule has begun, but much more remains to come. The rule of God, he said, is like seed already sown in the ground; but 'the blade, the ear, the full grain' is still to come before the final harvest. Jesus also said that in his miracles the power, which really belongs to the future rule of God, is already at work in the world. 'If it is by the Spirit of God that I cast out demons,' he declared, 'then the kingdom of God *has* come upon you.' So the rule of God is something which is already being *given* to us. 'Fear not, little flock,' Jesus said to his first disciples, 'for it is your Father's good pleasure to give you the kingdom.'

This rule of God will be completed only in the future. It cannot now be described; it is hinted at in various pictures and symbols. Paul, for example, sketches God's complete purpose as 'his gathering of all things together into one in Christ', bringing the whole of creation into a unity like the radiating spokes of a wheel with Christ as the hub.

The Church, prayer and the kingdom

It is never said in the New Testament that we shall build the kingdom – perhaps this is to remind us of our dependence on God – but that we shall *receive* the kingdom. We must long for it, pray for it, and give ourselves to God so that he can use us to bring in his kingdom.

Jesus taught us to pray for the kingdom in the one special prayer he gave us. The Lord's prayer comes to us in slightly different versions in St Matthew and St Luke. In the former gospel it is not said, 'pray these words' but 'pray in this way'; so there the Lord's prayer is not so much a set form of prayer, but a suggested sequence for all our praying. Teresa of Avila said to her followers, 'To know how to pray the Lord's prayer well will show you how to pray all other prayers.'

In each of these two versions, the *pivot* of the prayer, as of all Jesus' teaching in the earliest gospels, is '*Thy kingdom come*'. The coming of God's rule, rather than our individual fellowship with God, is the primary aim of all our praying.

The preceding words of this prayer, 'Father, hallowed be your name', lead us to look to the Father in adoration and in confidence. This is an indispensable preparation. For unless we direct our mind and heart first to God himself, we shall be probably praying and working for our own kingdom, not for his.

Then the petitions in the Lord's prayer, which follow this pivot clause, grow out of it. For if we are praying for God's kingdom, then our wills need to be aligned to his will; we need food, our daily necessities; we need to be forgiven and to be delivered from evil.

This coming of the kingdom will involve a long struggle. The great evils in the world have to be challenged and driven out. We see this movement starting in Jesus in his life of love, his death and resurrection. There is much opposition still to overcome. I doubt if abstract principles – principles of human rights or even principles of his kingdom – will give us incentive and strength enough. It is personal devotion to and love for Jesus, human and divine, the inaugurator of the rule of God, that will alone be enough to keep us going.

For this great task God gives us progressively the power of the Spirit of Jesus. Paul uses for this the word *arrabon*, a commercial term used of the first instalment of some money you are going to be given, and also the guarantee that the rest of the money will come to you in the future. Paul says that we have already received the *arrabon* of the Spirit, and that God promises us more and more of the power of the Spirit, as we need it in our great task. Similarly Paul tells us we have already the *arrabon*, the first instalment, of the future rule of God, of the future 'gathering of all things in one in Christ'. We shall see its fulfilment in history or in eternity.

So in our experience of life together as Christians we have already a foretaste of the future rule of God in heaven. Paul says the same thing in his letter to the Philippians, using a different analogy. The city of Philippi took its origin from a settlement of soldiers from Rome itself. They did their best to reproduce the customs and ethos of Rome, their homeland; and they were called a 'colony' of Rome. In a similar way, Paul says that the Christians at Philippi form a 'colony (*politeuma*) of heaven'. So we too should reproduce in our local churches and groups the love and joy of heaven, our true homeland; and so we may attract others to God revealed in Jesus.

112

Action and prayer

What does the world need most? Action or prayer? Isn't that an over-simplified choice? Brother Roger put these questions to thirty-five thousand young people camping round the village of Taizé for their 1974 Council of Youth. He called on them for definite action to set men and women everywhere free from poverty and oppression.

He equally called them to contemplative praying, prayer with our hearts open to God. This prayer would bring to them, he said, two blessings – first, the love and strength they would need for this long struggle – and, secondly, the art of listening to God and also to others. True reformers do not arrogantly impose on others their own ideas. Ben Kingsley studied some old newsreels, while he was preparing to take the title role in the Gandhi film. What impressed him most was not the words the Mahatma spoke, nor how he modulated his voice, but the sensitive way he listened to each one who came to him.

Brother Roger has appropriately entitled one of his recent journals *Lutte et Contemplation*, social struggle *and* contemplation. These he said are 'The two poles between which we are to situate our whole existence'.

12

Prayer, Involvement, Leisure

It was one of the most beautiful journeys I have ever made – a hundred and sixty miles from Colombo on the coast to Bandarawela at 5,000 feet among the mountains in the centre of Sri Lanka. We saw tropical beaches with their palms, next the rice paddyfields with every conceivable tint of green, then tea plantations with women working in saris. We climbed to the uplands, something like our Pennines, but with lakes, waterfalls, rhododendrons and all sorts of flowers. Towering above us was the sharp Adam's Peak, a sacred mountain for Buddhists, Hindus and Christians.

I was travelling with the last of the English bishops of Colombo. We were wearing white cassocks. He pointed out to me the sights of interest. After a good lunch he nodded off to sleep. A polite, young Sinhalese beside me whispered, 'Is that the Bishop of Colombo? Is he soon to retire? Is he showing it all to you because you are going to be the next bishop?' I explained that I was in Sri Lanka giving courses only for a month and that the bishop and I were going up to his bungalow at Bandarawela to spend a couple of days together. There we were going to enjoy three things, which are so important for all of us in our everyday lives – praying, planning and leisure.

Prayer
We arranged our times of prayer. But what mattered most to both of us was the Practice of the Presence of God. It is so vital. I have spoken to you about it in various ways. You can choose the way that suits you. I have

tried to be realistic and practical. But have I made it sound a bit too tense? It is not so much our effort to remember and reach out to God. *The Practice of the Presence of God means that at every moment God himself is reaching out in his love to us.*

May I now share with you a small book that has brought this home to me – I had it with me in Sri Lanka. It is *The Sacrament of the Present Moment* by Jean-Pierre de Caussade, an obscure priest in the eighteenth century. For years he was an ordinary Jesuit schoolmaster. Then he went as chaplain to some Sisters in Nancy. Some of his letters and addresses to them circulated as secret papers during the French revolution, like Bonhoeffer's letters did in Nazi Germany. They have now been published and have made Père de Caussade 'the patron saint' for busy men and women of today.

The Quaker, Richard Foster, recommends them in his introduction to an American edition. He spent a long flight reading this book. 'The journey from the Pacific coast to the Atlantic', he wrote, 'was a long one, but the inward journey that I entered into that day was far greater.' And it has altered, he says, the whole spirit of his life, for it has shown him how to experience all his daily jobs as sacraments conveying God's love – 'teaching students, answering correspondence, playing with my boys, repairing broken window panes, paying bills, washing dishes', as he lists them.

All that Père de Caussade says about 'the sacrament of the present moment' is firmly built on the New Testament's fundamental truth not only that 'God loves' but that 'God is love', as the sun is heat. So God cannot stop radiating love, just as the sun cannot stop radiating heat – although God's love like the sun may sometimes be hidden from our eyes by clouds. Therefore God's love is coming to us through the events and duties of every successive moment. True, God does not send what is happening each moment: for example,

God did not send the boy's ball through Richard's window pane. Yet God's love was being radiated in that moment and wished to reach Richard in that moment. 'God', says de Caussade, 'makes of all things mysteries and sacraments of his love.' What is happening to us just now is the outward form of the sacrament of God's ever-present love – even though it looks strange to us; indeed in the holy sacrament itself our eating bread looks at first sight a strange way of receiving into our hearts the eternal love of God. So Père de Caussade goes on, 'Why should not every moment of our lives be a sort of communion with the divine love?' Now to receive God's love in this way hour by hour – and how valuable and strengthening this would be! – we need to train ourselves in two ways.

First, we have really to root ourselves in this truth that God is this continuously-radiated love. It is not enough to read about it. We need it to seep down into us through some meditative or contemplative praying.

Secondly, we have to *train ourselves* in the art of concentration in all our daily life. It is quite possible. We find, for example, we can concentrate when we are gripped by a book: or when we meet a close friend again after a long time. Or again, when we are actually receiving holy communion, we are sometimes so absorbed in it that for the moment we forget everything else. So we have to cultivate our capacity for concentration. Père de Caussade recommends: 'We must cut off all more distant views, we must confine ourselves to the duty of the present moment without thinking of what preceded it or what will follow it.' And he gives his reason: 'The duties of each moment are shadows beneath which the divine action lies concealed.'

Jesus says, 'Don't be anxious about tomorrow'. And de Caussade writes 'Try not to let apprehension about the future or regret about the past flood over into your present living and make you miserable.' We shall then be less harassed and less exhausted. He tells us we shan't always succeed; and one of the charming things about him is that he admits that he didn't either. He was called to leave Nancy to become superior of a Jesuit house at Perpignan. He didn't manage to follow his own good advice; on the contrary, he grumbled and complained that he had no qualifications for the job. It involved all kinds of business which he could not understand. He also disliked VIP visits; yet on his arrival the bishop, steward, king's lieutenant, sheriff, garrison officer all called on him. But afterwards – to his own surprise – he could write to one of the nuns: 'I remain calm and in peace in the midst of a thousand worries and complications in which I should have expected to be overwhelmed.' He had come back to his own teaching about the present moment.

What he asks of us is not a reluctant resignation to the all-but-inevitable, but rather a confident, hour-by-hour placing of ourselves in God's loving hands. This is how Jesus himself lived. And we through the sacrament of the present moment can share in Jesus' confidence in the Father – in the hurly-burly of life and in our leisure.

Involvement

At his bungalow the bishop and I planned how far I should be involved in the life of Sri Lanka. We all need to pray and to consult others about our involvement in life. We don't want to spend our time or our money irresponsibly. God doesn't mean us to rush about trying to do something for everybody or to give to every charitable appeal until our health – or our purses – are exhausted. We need to plan how we spend our money and our time.

We must also remember that Christian responsibilities are entrusted, not to us, but to the whole Church, the Body of Christ. God, as Paul says, has apportioned to us, as members of his serving Church, each our own particular and differing gifts. Let us study

117

some special areas of service for which our gifts fit us, and let us serve there with skill and gladness.

Our involvement will, I suppose, cover our job, our immediate circle and the wider world. Our job is very important; we glanced at its deep significance, symbolized in the offering of bread at the eucharist.

Our care for family and friends, church and neighbourhood

After a hard day's work, many feel like 'taking it easy and putting their feet up'. I'll write soon about relaxation. Yet we must, I think, do some planning of our free time. Our families and friends must come first. We're spending our time and effort and patience well, when we are trying really to get on with one another as friends, partners and families. For God wants our homes and friendships to bring his reign of love into our neighbourhood.

How many there are round about us, young and old, who need companionship, human and divine. Our Christian congregations and groups are called by God to offer this fellowship to others. To do that our churches and groups need to stand out clearly as centres of love and joy; and this requires time and thought.

Wider concerns

Then there are calls for action in the problems of unemployment, of our inner cities, of the Third World and of peace. We must not close our eyes; we must *do* something. We Christians should agree with Karl Marx on at least one point – we are not here to interpret the world, but 'to *change* the world'. Bertrand Russell, lifelong atheist, also said, 'What the world needs is Christian love and compassion.' Justice is love distributed.

First, we must try to find accurate information. Then our battle is in the area of public opinion. As Bishop

John Taylor says, 'Nothing can achieve change in policies without a profound reorientation of public opinion.'

Next, we may need to make time to share in social action perhaps to help unemployed school-leavers or to care for old people living alone. We should interest ourselves too and participate in party politics. There are sincere Christians in all parties. William Temple, who did so much to alert people to such issues, said, 'The Church lays down principles; the Christian citizen applies them'; and he added, 'The Church itself cannot say how it is to be done; but it is called to say it must be done.'

Then, in all our social and political activities we, as Christians, must serve others in *depth*. We must try to enter into the feelings of our fellow-men and women, their joys and distresses. But we must not see them only as so many hundreds of idle hands or as so many thousands of hungry mouths. Our *basic* motivation goes deeper – *they are all part of us*; each one, equally with us, is made in the image of God, each one constantly loved by God in Christ, each needing to be linked to God and to one another by love. It is this deep motivation which will keep us going. We shall not be discouraged by apparent lack of results or even by outbreaks of violence. Even evil men and women among them are our brothers and sisters in the one, God-loved, human family. Each one is at least potentially a member of Christ and of his body. And did not Jesus say when we visit the starving and the prisoner we visit him?

So whenever we can do practical service for them, we must do it – without, as we have said, neglecting those close to us. The one service we can always give them is prayer. But if we make prayer a substitute for available action, then this prayer is a 'cop-out'.

Our prayer cannot be confined to those we are actually meeting. We are to make intercessions and

119

thanksgivings, the first letter to Timothy says, for all men, specially for those with heavy responsibilities.

I am often asked, 'But does this kind of prayer, prayer "at a distance", make any difference?' Christians right from New Testament times have believed that it does. I have already explained how – through the words and life of Jesus – I have become convinced that, because God is love, he can never be unresponsive to us and so he always does something. How he answers – or, to use a more satisfactory word, how he uses our prayers – we often do not know. He does not seem always to send rain to areas of drought, and never does he topple tyrants and oppressors with thunderbolts. Through our prayers I believe he moves the hearts of men and women at home and abroad to give themselves in service to those in need. Whenever we truly intercede, I am sure, as we have seen, he gradually by his Spirit transforms *us*, so that we no longer block the universal current of his love but transmit and share it.

We also saw that genuine intercession means putting ourselves into the hands of his love for him to use us. This may mean giving money, or persuading others to become involved in action with us. How much further this may lead us in the venture of service we can't tell. Perhaps this is why we sometimes do not *really* pray.

Leisure

'Let us go off by ourselves to some place where we can be alone', Jesus said to his disciples, 'and we can rest for a while.' So it was with the two of us in our enjoyable walks at Bandarawela. Everyone needs some free – really free – time. In it we may perhaps refresh our bodies, cultivate our aesthetical gifts and enrich our faith.

It is by giving him our *bodies* in his service that Paul tells us to express our gratitude to God. God created our bodies. God used the human body of Jesus to reveal his eternal love. So to keep as physically fit as we

120

can is part of being a Christian. How then should we regularly exercise and relax our bodies, so that we can – through our bodies and minds – bring his reign of love into our present world?

Leisure is time to discover or develop those hidden gifts, that can bring balance into our lives; to look for a hobby in congenial company, if you work largely on your own; to try some skill in the arts, if your work is scientific or intellectual. 'Reading a poem or a novel, looking at a picture or hearing some music,' says Richard Harries, a well-known broadcaster, 'can shake us out of dull routine and give new zest to our love of God.'

To me it is a delight to read in my spare time a little of the letters and the writings of men and women of faith and prayer; they have become to me real friends. A 'spiritual guide' could suggest which books might be suitable to us at the present stage of our journey and how to read them with discrimination. If we are too fascinated by the 'latest book', we might remember the words of Dean Inge of St Paul's: 'He who marries himself to modern ideas may find himself a widower tomorrow.' On the other hand, some of the spiritual classics may disappoint us, if we forget the social conditions and attitudes of their times. Many of these books have at least traces of a manichean outlook on life in which matter, the human body and its feelings are regarded as second rate. The Carmelite, Ruth Burrows, corrects this manichean teaching and writes: 'A Christian joyfully accepts his bodiliness, knowing that he can go to God only through the body and that God comes to him through his body.' At the same time there has always been a genuine and healthy tradition of self-discipline in the Christian life.

Yet we learn to pray and love God, not through reading books, but through praying and loving. 'You learn to study by studying,' Francis de Sales said, 'to play the lute by playing, to dance by dancing, to swim

121

by swimming; and just so you learn to love God and man by loving. All those who think to learn in any other way deceive themselves.'

Adult appreciation of the Bible and our Christian faith
Several of my friends find two half hours of reading in the week or an hour at weekends something they really look forward to. In this way all of us can over the years gradually make up the gaps in our earlier spiritual education. It is also a stimulating way of preparing ourselves to help others, whenever an opportunity comes.

I am speaking of the scriptures and our Christian faith, understood and appreciated in an adult way, *grasped and lived on our journey in today's world.* We can't be like camels. They start off with a great drink at an oasis and then live on that water for the rest of the long way across the sandy desert. We on our journey need to be in mind and heart continually refreshed – and in up-to-date ways.

I have spoken already about 'Bible-praying'. Let us look now at its essential complement, Bible-reading or Bible-study. It is a contemporary, adult understanding of the scriptures that we need. We have to steer our way between two extremes. Some modern people dismiss the Bible as irrelevant and a great deal of it as legendary. Others on the contrary try to use it as an encyclopaedia with pat answers to all questions. I myself agree with John Stott, an evangelical observer of the modern scene; we don't want 'proof-texting', that is, trying to settle questions by quoting single texts, isolated out of their original setting.

What matters vitally to us is to grasp with mind as well as heart the fundamental truths in the scriptures – about God as he really is and about our human nature. How were the first Christians led to accept the truth that we see God and his love when we look at Jesus and his love in the gospels? And how did the Spirit enable them to see its full implications for their praying and living in the world?

And God's love in the New Testament – let me say again – is always an understanding love and a love sometimes as strong as an autumn gale. Unless the gale blows off old dying leaves and dead wood, there will be no fresh green in spring. Without the gale of God's love, there will be no springtime in our lives.

To grasp all this we need some planned reading of the gospels and the other New Testament books. And we cannot understand how the minds of the first Christians worked, unless we know how they were influenced by Old Testament writers. And remember that for decades the Old Testament was the only Bible the early Christians had.

It is these basic questions about how we know the real God that shape and mould our praying and our living now. They are the questions which are being discussed round about us every day in an England, where there are more Muslims than Methodists. You and I need to try also to understand these other faiths.

Equally vital for us is to know – and to be able to explain to others – how we understand the depths of our nature as men and women. Modern psychology and sociology tell us much. But it is through the study of the scriptures, particularly the words and life of Jesus, that we come to a firm grasp of what our human nature really is. We see that we cannot mature into our true selves – and so do our best service in today's world – without a living fellowship both with God and also with one another. So we need to read and reflect systematically on this, each of us in whatever way is most helpful. There are also many ways now in which we can discuss these things together.

There are modern ethical and social questions which the Bible does not answer, because in those days they were never asked. But invaluable light is thrown on them through these basic biblical truths about God, and about men and women too. We can exist but we cannot be fully alive without God and without one another. Again we need not only to know this, but also to be able to talk over its social implications with others.

So then let us never hesitate to ask for good advice on how to read and reflect on the scriptures in these ways. A stimulating book to start on is, I think, *Believing makes Sense* by a lively Dutch Dominican, Lucas Grollenberg.

Special weekends

A feature of modern life is going away for special weekends – painting weekends, musical weekends, marriage enrichment weekends. I would like to recommend two other kinds.

You might consider going to a weekend workshop on prayer. I have conducted many of these weekends. We not only hear about meditation and prayer, but we actually try, with advice, to do them together. It is quite a help, if we wish, modestly to share with others our experience of prayer, and perhaps find to our encouragement that our difficulties are not peculiarly our own. These weekends are offered to people at every stage of the life of meditation and prayer. Some friends of mine in Australia have even arranged meditation weekends for agnostics.

Many people find another great help is a silent weekend retreat. Its purpose is not so much to give you more instruction on prayer, but through the Spirit to deepen your personal companionship with God. If someone offered their tiny weekend cottage to a busy, exhausted husband and wife, how quickly they would jump at the offer and make arrangements! When they arrived, they wouldn't want to go to the village pub and meet other people. They would want to be together, sharing their thoughts, and enjoying one another's company. Their love would grow deeper; they would probably be better parents and better neighbours when they returned home. It is like that between God and ourselves in a retreat. There is a simple programme with times of worship and short talks designed to deepen our love with God. We need an annual retreat, I think, as much as an annual holiday.

In ordinary life we need to plan – to revise for an examination, to meet a publisher's deadline, or even to go on a family camping holiday. It is the same in our life of faith and prayer. But we must not be inflexible in our plans. The Holy Spirit can use our unexpected hunches. Once when my engagement book appeared to be packed about the time of Lent, there came a surprise invitation to give a long weekend course on the Continent. Normally I would have said 'Sorry, impossible.' But for some reason I hesitated and prayed about it. I could not dismiss it from my mind. I wrote for some small modifications in the suggested programme. When these were arranged I said 'Yes'.

And what a good thing I went. It showed me a fresh way of retreats. It introduced me to many new friends. It turned out to be a landmark in my journey through life.

13

Journeying on in Time and Eternity

One of the thrills of life is to fly in a small plane. After conducting some retreats in Dunedin in the south island of New Zealand, which combines Swiss alps and Norwegian fjords, I took two short flights with only the pilot, two other passengers and myself. One day we flew from the Hermitage at the foot of Mount Cook and landed on the Tasman glacier; in a swerve on the way back we felt that we could almost stretch out a hand and touch a gigantic icefall. On the other day we flew down a very narrow fjord between two enormous walls of rock. The plane needed skilful manoeuvring to land on a tiny airstrip near the base of the 5,000-foot Mitre Peak, which rises sheer out of the ocean.

Both flights were exciting, but a little frightening. What might happen if we had been caught in a sudden squall of wind! But life is *always* more insecure than we think. Every day we read of fatal accidents and heart attacks; and we quietly assume it will always be someone else and not us. Yet we must not be anxious.

But we wonder about what will happen to us – or perhaps, even more, to those we love – after death. If I may speak personally, the only thing I can feel sure about in the life to come is what has been said by Jesus. He spoke so clearly about the life beyond death. He said, you remember, to a thief who was dying beside him on his cross, 'I promise you that today you will be in Paradise with me', implying that they would in some way recognize one another.

Human words cannot describe the life to come, but that does not make us doubt its reality. Similarly human words cannot describe our experiences of music and love, yet we are sure of their reality.

Sometimes people fear that some of their departed loved ones may not receive this future blessing because of some serious fault in their lives or because of their lack of faith in God. First we must remember that, as Paul said, only God can judge, because God alone knows what has gone on inside them, and perhaps they made far more effort than any of us knew. Some of those who have called themselves agnostics or even atheists have not rejected God, but only inadequate ideas of God; and so they may have taken a step on the road towards the real God. And in this life we have already experienced how we have been helped and purified by someone truly loving us. So God's love may prepare and purify us all before we receive the full joy of heaven.

Eternal life, here and to come
We must not make the mistake of thinking that life here and the life to come are quite different from one another. When the scriptures and specially St John's gospel speak of life eternal, *zoe aionios*, they do not mean only heaven. Life eternal, this gospel says, consists of 'knowing God and Jesus Christ whom he has sent to us'. And this 'knowing' is, as we have seen already, knowing in the deepest way through being loved by God and responding to him in love through the Spirit. Through this mutual love we already have life eternal now. In another place it says quite simply. 'He, who believes, *has* life eternal.' Life eternal reaches its fullness in heaven but we begin to enjoy it now in our life of love and involvement on earth, in spite of difficulties and perplexities. In the same way mature human love is our early love, purified through difficulties, deepened and enriched. So how vital it is that we should deepen our fellowship with God here and now by confidence and real prayer.

127

We have already noticed that our concern with the future life should not make us care less about conditions in this world, but on the contrary more; because this life is intended to be not only something very valuable in itself, but also preparation and training for the life to come.

The life to come, corporate

We try to grow in fellowship here and now, for example, by our learning to forgive one another, and this should prepare us for the deeper fellowship of the life to come. The Lord's words to the dying thief show that the life to come is a corporate life. The symbolic language in the Bible about heaven as a city and as a banquet points to the same thing. So heaven is not being alone with God, but it is being in God with one another.

But looking forward to this future joy is for some people rather clouded over. There may be family quarrels never fully resolved or forgiven. They may also remember the sincere, but narrow views of older relatives and friends, for example, about the interpretation of the Bible. Those whom we shall meet will have changed as we have done. The life to come is not a passive state like sleep. It is a life of development. When Jesus says of the God of Abraham, Isaac and Jacob that 'He is the God not of the dead, but of the living', he implies that these ancestors are not dead men, but are still living.

So our departed friends and relatives go on living in the light and love of God himself. So they must be developing and growing in love, in forgiveness and in width of understanding. We cannot possibly imagine what these future reunions will be, but I am convinced that because they will be reunions within God's love, they will be reunions of acceptance and joy. 'Welcome one another, as Christ has welcomed you' will be even more true there than here.

128

Life eternal begins now and blossoms out in the life to come. I treasure a letter from that close, evangelical friend of mine, Max Warren, of whom I have spoken. He wrote to me not long before his death, 'Perhaps because I am growing old I have become increasingly aware of my indebtedness to countless people who are now in heaven. I am as sure as I am of my writing to you that some of these poeple have been allowed by God to continue to minister to me in all kinds of situations. This, as I see it, is a little of the overflow of God's great disclosure of love. What I have never believed is that in God's great purpose those on the other side of death are unemployed.'

It would be a strength and a joy for us all if we could share with our Eastern Orthodox brothers and sisters their deep sense of continuing closeness to our own dear departed ones as well as to the saints of all the ages; this closeness is conveyed by the very expressive Russian word *sobornost*, 'togetherness'.

Let me add a personal word of my own. When I was a young man, my mother died; I could never cease to love her; and because I loved, I could never cease to pray. Of course I did not know her precise needs. But I was – and am – sure she in God's light and love is still becoming an even more wonderful woman. So day by day I go on praying for her. She continues, I am sure, to love me; and because she loves, she still prays for me. Years ago in our home together I used to ask for and rely on her prayers. And I ask her now to sustain me by her prayers as I continue my journey of growing into the man and into the priest God means me still to become.

Envoy

As I come to the end of another book, I sit quietly and pray for many I have met on my journeys and for those who may read this book. What do I long for – for them, and for myself? Prayer that is real.

A dear friend of mine, after a very active life, lay dying with a quiet, joyful confidence. As her strength was ebbing away, she said, 'There is now only love left to me to live on.'

In spite of all our insecurities in the world of today, you and I, like Laurens van der Post and so many others, can journey with that same confidence, because we too have that same love to live on – love disclosed and brought to us in Jesus. That love we can bring within ourselves by prayer that is real, the prayer, which happens whenever those two mysteries overlap, the wonderful mystery who is you and the supreme mystery who is God.

This is the prayer that never stops – unceasing prayer sustained by whatever 'special' times of prayer we can plan and manage.

We need flexibility and spontaneity.

But to fail to plan is to plan to fail.

And now I must try afresh, with God's love, to live what I have written.

FOR FURTHER READING

J. L. G. Balado, *The Story of Taizé*, Mowbray, Oxford, 1985

V. Brümmer, *What are We Doing when We Pray? A Philosophical Inquiry*, SCM Press, 1984

Ruth Burrows, *To Believe in Jesus*, Sheed and Ward, 1978

J.-P. de Caussade, *The Sacrament of the Present Moment* (translated by K. Muggeridge), Collins Fount, 1981; and Harper and Row Publishers Inc., San Francisco, USA, 1984

Cloud of Unknowing (translated by C. Wolters), Penguin, 1975

J. Dominian, *The Capacity to Love*, Darton, Longman and Todd, 1985

J. D. G. Dunn, *The Evidence for Jesus*, SCM Press, 1985

A. Ecclestone, *Yes to God*, Darton, Longman and Todd, 1975

C. Elliott, *Praying the Kingdom: Towards a Political Spirituality*, Darton, Longman and Todd, 1985

Faith in the City: a Call for Action, Church House Publishing, London, 1985

R. Faricy S. J., *Praying for Inner Healing*, SCM Press, 1979

G. Gutierrez, *We Drink from Our Own Wells*, SCM Press, 1984

R. Harries, *Prayer and the Pursuit of Happiness*, Collins Fount, 1985

Brother Lawrence, *The Practice of the Presence of God*, Mowbray, Oxford, 1980

K. Leech, *True God: an Exploration in Spiritual Theology*, SPCK, 1985

R. Llewelyn, *Prayer and Contemplation*, Fairacres, Oxford, 1980

T. Merton, *Contemplative Prayer*, Darton, Longman and Todd, 1973

S. Moore, *Let this Mind be in You*, Darton, Longman and Todd, 1985

Henri J. M. Nouwen, *The Way of the Heart: Desert Spirituality and Contemporary Ministry*, Darton, Longman and Todd, 1981

Helen Oppenheimer, *Incarnation and Immanence*, Hodder and Stoughton, 1973

M. Basil Pennington, *Centering Prayer*, Doubleday, New York, 1982

J. Stott, *Issues facing Christians Today*, Marshalls, 1984

A. and B. Ulanov, *Primary Speech: a Psychology of Prayer*, SCM Press, 1985

K. Ward, *The Living God*, SPCK, .1984

Several series of daily Bible-reading notes can be obtained from The Bible Reading Fellowship (2 Elizabeth Street, London SW1W 9RQ) and also on more conservative lines from The Scripture Union (130 City Road, London EC1V 2NJ).

Places and dates of retreats are published each year by The Association for Promoting Retreats (Liddon House, 24 South Audley Street, London W1Y 5DL).